TONJA ENGEN

Tonja's table

MENUS AND RECIPES FOR EVERY OCCASION.

ISBN 13: 978-1-945769-20-7

Library of Congress Catalog Number: Available upon request.

Printed in the United States of America
First Printing: 2017
21 20 19 18 17 5 4 3 2 1

Photography By:
Jenifer Williams, Ampersand Photography & Design - www.ampersandphotodesign.com
Isabel M. Subtil, Isabel Subtil Photography - www.isabelsubtil.com
Clay Johnston, Sprung Interactive - www.madebysprung.com
Bonjwing Lee, Bonjwing Photography - www.bonjwing.com

Cover and interior design by James Monroe Design, LLC.

Published by W.I. Creative Publishing, an imprint of Wise Ink Creative Publishing..

W.I. Creative Publishing
837 Glenwood Avenue
wiseinkpub.com

To order, visit seattlebookcompany.com or call (734) 426-6248.
Reseller discounts available.

To Greg,
for all your faith in me,
all the date-night dinner adventures,
hours as my prep-cook in the kitchen,
and your endless patience and love.
You are my favorite person to dream with.

CONTENTS

INTRODUCTION

When I set out to write a cookbook I had two things in mind: to share delicious recipes you would want to make over and over again, and to help make cooking more fun in the kitchen. The friends and family in my life have given me inspiration to do this. They have let me tell my story through food and cooking. This is my passion. I love to think about food. I love to talk about food. While eating one meal, I am thinking about the next. I read cookbooks for therapy. My husband laughs because I read them like novels. (I once read Julia Child's *My Life in France* beginning to end on the drive home to Minnesota from Yellowstone.)

I wrote this cookbook from a food lover's point of view. Some recipes are indulgent, others are simple, and a few are complex. The common thread is that these recipes all taste incredible. One thing my *Tonja's Table* blog readers love is that I don't skimp on flavor. Flavor is a *must* for me. I decided to write an occasions cookbook that is chock-full of flavor and fun because when I polled my friends and family, they told me their biggest challenge was not knowing what to make for their events.

I wanted to create a cookbook that would be your companion in the kitchen. Nothing makes me happier than when friends or blog readers tell me they enjoyed dinner with friends, they were a hit at the potluck, or their holiday was spectacular because of a *Tonja's Table* recipe.

As I look back, I can see that my food obsession started when I was a kid. My parents would watch me over-order every single time we went out to eat because I just loved food so much. (Picture a little blonde girl with blue eyes bigger than her stomach.) My friends would argue that I still over-order, but now I share.

There were other pivotal food moments for me as well—both good and bad. (Everyone has a fire story, right?) The deal was sealed, however, when I studied abroad. What I learned, or maybe stumbled into, was the idea that food isn't just about eating. I learned that food is about tradition and culture, that every place puts its own spin on food, and that meals are meant to be shared experiences. Like an addict, I couldn't wait to find the next one. Meals became my sightseeing guide to cultures and their traditions, and I couldn't get enough. There weren't enough meals in a day! Oh, to have that metabolism again.

Necessity played a role in my love affair with food, too. When my husband Greg and I were first married, one of our favorite date nights was going out to eat. It was perfect. I didn't cook much in those days—going out to eat was fun, and it made no mess to clean up at home. All that changed when we had two toddlers and found ourselves spending more nights in. We had to get creative with date nights, so our evenings at home centered on food. In those days you couldn't get much more than pizza delivered, so cooking was our only option. It was also a great way to bribe our friends to hang out with us at home when we couldn't get out.

Before I knew it, this cooking thing was growing into a full-blown hobby. I found myself swapping novels for cookbooks and researching and experimenting with recipes every chance I got. As I do with most things, I dove in headfirst, and once I was swimming, I couldn't stop. I found it exhilarating to cook something a famous chef had made or to use an ingredient that I had to learn how to pronounce. I could relive a special meal that I'd had in Europe or a favorite restaurant by making it! I could recreate memories in my own home anytime I wanted to.

Now, when I plan my weekend, it's often about what new restaurant I can try. Dining out at a new place is like attending a premier for me. I can't wait to experience it. Some people ogle rock stars and movie moguls. I am giddy over chefs. I thrive on learning new food trends and can't wait to try them. I collect food experiences the way some people collect art.

But unlike art, food is accessible to everyone. It doesn't just hang on a wall in a room you don't use. Good food entices us to gather around and eat and talk and laugh and create memories we'll recall years from now. There's a reason we congregate in the kitchen at every party no matter where we strategically place the food. That's my favorite part of cooking: making and sharing food with others and seeing happy, relaxed faces at the table.

In some ways I feel as if I am still traveling; this food hobby has turned into such an adventure. In fact, it has landed me in the last place I ever thought I would be—here, writing an intro to my own cookbook.

I started my food blog, *Tonja's Table*, after many years of home cooking and owning a small catering business. I received so many recipe requests that I started putting recipes on my blog. Occasions, by far, cause the most cooking angst for my readers. So this cookbook is for them—and for anyone who wants to have a trusted recipe for any occasion.

When you don't know what to make, let this cookbook help make your life easier. I want this book to be like having your best friend in the kitchen with you—someone who always has your back and makes cooking fun because the hard part is done for you. I have spent the last twenty years perfecting recipes so you don't have to. You'll always know what to cook for what occasion, and you know the recipes will work and taste fantastic. You don't have to be a professional chef to make these crazy-good meals. I'm so excited for you to try them. Once you do, I know you will feel like a star in the kitchen in no time.

I have had my share of mishaps in twenty years of cooking. And the fact that I love to entertain means I sometimes have them with other people around. ("Oops! I forgot to put the sauce on. Oh well, let's use it as a dip!") But this is the beauty of food: even a fail can be fun, and if you're really lucky, you may get a delicious new recipe out of it. I also try not to take myself to seriously in the kitchen. That's why my husband likes to call me "Lucy" (as in *I Love Lucy*). He never knows what he's going to get when he pulls into the garage after work.

My husband came home one evening and most—actually, *all*—of the neighborhood kids were shooting a movie at our house. It was an all-day affair, complete with lights, cameras, and of course lots of props in the backyard. It was break time for the neighborhood of actors, so I decided to feed the movie crew with gourmet burgers, special sauce, and homemade potato chips. (Yep, I have a deep fryer.) I got those cute little baskets you get at the drive-ins and made it all fun and restaurant-like. And yes, my husband smiled politely and shook his head on his way through the kitchen.

I hope this book is a great first (or second, or third) step toward getting the fun back in food for you. I encourage everyone to cook, no matter their skill level or any frustrations they've had in the past. Remember: food is about relationships, not perfection. My hope is to get everyone to try new things in the kitchen and *love it*.

I've organized this book by occasion, with a menu for each one. But feel free to mix and match the recipes however you like.

So dive in, have fun, and best of luck on all your kitchen adventures.

XOXO,

Tonja

PS: You will not find a lot of desserts in my cookbook. Baking is too detailed for me. This skill skipped a generation in our family. My mom and my daughter are amazing bakers. Buy their cookbook when it comes out.

One

ENTERTAINING AND PARTIES

When Greg and I were first married, I had grand plans for weekly dinner parties and fanciful evenings around the dinner table. I mistakenly chose recipes I had never tried before and cooking techniques that were beyond my "new bride" abilities. I was obsessed with making coconut shrimp at the time (it was all the rage) and some kind of mango rice. And for some reason I thought a homemade banana cream pie fit in the mix, too. I knew nothing about food pairing, and I didn't bother to prep the shrimp beforehand. So to the horror of my guests, they ended up peeling and deveining shrimp for what seemed like hours. Worse, when I finally went to fry them, my oil was too hot, so I rushed the shrimp out of the pan, splattered oil everywhere, and started a "small" fire on our new stovetop. Fortunately, my commonsensical husband came to the rescue and we avoided a big disaster.

After that fateful night, I learned lots of things about entertaining. The biggest lesson: plan, plan, plan. Plan your menu, plan your table, plan your steps, and prep as much as you can. This way you will actually enjoy your own dinner party! Making your guests comfortable is the number one rule. Period.

The truth is, nobody wants a stuffy dinner party. Fancy? Sometimes. But stuffy? Never. Your guests want to laugh, indulge, and have a reprieve from their long week. Your friends want to share stories, unwind, and go home feeling loved and satisfied. That's it. Forget about the dust on your coffee table. That's what makes your home real and comfortable—not a new fancy kitchen and not a ten-course meal.

When entertaining guests, I asked several friends to share their biggest challenges. The resounding answer was "I'm not sure what to make," followed by "I don't want to be cooking when my guests arrive. It's too stressful and distracting." The entertaining menus that follow will help you get more done ahead of time. Some recipes are more elaborate than others, but all are equally delicious.

Casual Dinner Party
(THAT LOOKS REALLY HARD)

MENU

Greek Salmon with Israeli Couscous and Vodka-Spiked Yogurt Dill Sauce

---

This recipe is easy enough for a weeknight meal and fancy enough for a casual dinner with friends. I absolutely love the Greek flavors of lemon, feta, and kalamata olives. You could use some chicken or shrimp instead of salmon, and it would be just as delicious. Dollop the yogurt over the top of the salmon and couscous before serving.

Israeli couscous, sometimes called pearl couscous, consists of small, round pasta granules made from semolina and wheat flour. Israeli couscous is twice as big as regular couscous and is toasted rather than dried. This gives it a nutty flavor, a sturdy composition, and a chewy bite, helping it stand up to the sauce.

If you make the couscous ahead, drizzle it with olive oil and stir right before serving. This will loosen up the couscous.

GREEK SALMON
WITH ISRAELI COUSCOUS AND VODKA-SPIKED YOGURT DILL SAUCE

Servings: 4 to 6

For the salmon:

1 to 2 pounds salmon

2 tablespoons olive oil

2 tablespoons Greek seasoning (found at most grocers)

Salt and black pepper, to taste

For the couscous:

½ cup chicken broth

1 cup water

2 teaspoons minced garlic

1 cup Israeli couscous

½ cup chopped sun-dried tomatoes

½ cup sliced kalamata olives

½ cup crumbled feta cheese

2 teaspoons dried oregano

1 teaspoon ground black pepper

¼ cup white wine vinegar

2 tablespoons fresh lemon juice

¼ cup olive oil

For the sauce:

1 cup Greek yogurt

2 tablespoons vodka

2 tablespoons fresh-squeezed lemon juice

2 tablespoons freshly chopped dill

Salt and black pepper, to taste

Directions

Brush salmon with olive oil. Sprinkle with Greek seasoning and salt and pepper. Bake at 350°F for 20 to 25 minutes, depending on thickness of salmon.

To cook the couscous, pour the chicken broth and water into a saucepan, stir in the garlic, and bring to a boil. Stir in the couscous, cover the pan, and remove from heat. Allow the couscous to stand until all the liquid has been absorbed, 5 to 10 minutes; when done, fluff with a fork. Allow the couscous to cool to room temperature.

In a large serving bowl, lightly toss the couscous, sun-dried tomatoes, olives, and feta cheese. Mix the oregano, pepper, vinegar, and lemon juice in a small bowl, then pour over the couscous mixture. Toss again, then drizzle up to ¼ cup of olive oil over couscous and toss again. Adjust seasonings to taste.

To make the sauce, mix yogurt, vodka, lemon juice, and dill in a small serving dish. Season with salt and pepper and set aside.

To serve, place a scoop of couscous on a plate. Place salmon over the couscous and dollop with yogurt sauce.

Oscar-Worthy Cocktail Party

MENU

Crispy Cocktail Ribs with Madeira Wine Sauce

Baked Artichoke Dip with Roasted Red Peppers and Green Chilies

Spicy Thai Grilled Shrimp

Crab Cakes with Remoulade Sauce

Roast Beef Crostini with Horseradish Spread

Friends often ask me how many appetizers they should have for a cocktail party. As a general rule, if I'm not serving a main course, I plan for eight to ten appetizers per person for a party lasting longer than three hours and a variety of about six different appetizers. I always have a mix of meats, seafood, veggies, and dips, and the recipes I've included for this menu cover these categories in a delicious way.

Any butcher can cut the ribs for you. And remember, the secret to ribs is to start them at a high temp, then reduce the heat and cook them low and slow. That way they will be crispy on the outside and tender on the inside.

Pork seasoning and cornstarch make the ribs flavorful and crispy while they bake, and the sauce is so scrumptious you can dip just about anything in it. I like to serve these ribs with a plate of fresh veggies on the side. The artichoke dip recipe was inspired from the old Loring Café in Minneapolis. It's hands down the best artichoke dip out there. When you set out the shrimp, be careful; guests will elbow you for the last one. My secret ingredient in the crab cakes is potato chips—who would've thought?

CRISPY COCKTAIL RIBS
WITH MADEIRA WINE SAUCE

Servings: 30 pieces

For the ribs:

3 pounds lean pork spareribs or baby back ribs, cut into 2-inch lengths

Salt and black pepper, to taste

¼ cup Lunds & Byerlys Signature Pork Blend seasoning or any pork seasoning

¼ cup cornstarch

For the sauce:

1 ounce blue cheese

¼ cup Madeira wine

1 cup mayonnaise

1 cup sour cream

2 cloves garlic, minced

2 shallots, minced

Salt and black pepper, to taste

1 teaspoon Tabasco sauce

2 teaspoons Worcestershire sauce

Zest of 1 lemon

Directions

Preheat oven to 425°F. Place ribs in a large bowl. Season with salt, pepper, and pork seasoning. Add cornstarch and toss lightly with hands. This will create a crispy crust. Place on a foil-lined cookie sheet and bake 30 minutes. Then turn down to 300°F and bake another 45 minutes to 1 hour.

Combine all sauce ingredients except zest and mix until smooth. Add zest and gently stir. Season to taste if needed. You can make the sauce up to 5 days in advance.

BAKED ARTICHOKE DIP

WITH ROASTED RED PEPPERS AND GREEN CHILIES

Directions

Combine all ingredients in a large bowl and stir until all incorporated. Pour dip into an oven-safe dish. Bake at 350°F until bubbly and slightly golden brown on top, 30 to 35 minutes.

Brush baguette slices with olive oil and toast in oven at 400°F for 10 to 12 minutes or until lightly golden. Serve alongside dip.

Servings: 20

1 cup mayonnaise

1 cup shredded Parmesan cheese

1 ½ cups shredded mozzarella

1 can (15 ounces) artichoke hearts, chopped

1 tablespoon lemon juice

1 clove garlic, minced

¾ can (4.25 ounces) chopped black olives

¼ cup chopped roasted red pepper

4 scallions, finely sliced

1 can (4.25 ounces) diced green chilies

1 loaf French bread, sliced

SPICY THAI GRILLED SHRIMP

Directions

Place the shrimp in a zip-loc bag. Place the coconut milk, lime juice, fish sauce, sriracha, garlic, ginger, and salt in a medium bowl and whisk to combine. Pour the marinade over the shrimp and marinate for 30 minutes and up to 4 hours.

Preheat the grill to medium-high. Remove the shrimp from the marinade and skewer. Brush oil on the grill and add shrimp. Grill 2–3 minutes per side or until firm and opaque, basting shrimp once. Remove from grill to a platter and squeeze a bit of fresh lime juice over shrimp. Serve hot.

Servings: 24 Shrimp

2 pounds jumbo shrimp, peeled and deveined

2 cups coconut milk

⅓ cup sriracha sauce (more if you want it spicier)

¼ cup lime juice

¼ cup Thai fish sauce

1 tablespoon minced garlic

1 tablespoon minced ginger

1 tablespoon kosher salt

Metal or bamboo skewers (soaked in cold water)

Vegetable oil

CRAB CAKES
WITH REMOULADE SAUCE

Servings: 20 Crab Cakes

For crab cakes:

1 bag plain potato chips, crushed

1 teaspoon dry mustard

1 tablespoon Old Bay seasoning

¼ teaspoon black pepper

2 bunches scallions, chopped

1 egg, beaten

½ cup mayonnaise

1 tablespoon Worcestershire sauce

4 cans (6.5 ounces) lump crabmeat

For remoulade sauce:

1 cup mayonnaise

1 tablespoon Dijon mustard

2 teaspoons tomato paste

1 teaspoon minced shallot

¼ cup minced dill pickle

½ teaspoon Worcestershire sauce

1 teaspoon Old Bay seasoning

1 tablespoon minced fresh flat-leaf parsley

Directions

Preheat oven to 400°F.

Mix all ingredients for crab cakes together and shape into silver-dollar–size patties. Brush both sides with butter. Bake 15 to 20 minutes.

To make remoulade sauce, mix all ingredients together and refrigerate. Serve with crab cakes.

ROAST BEEF CROSTINI

WITH HORSERADISH SPREAD

Directions

Add oil and butter to skillet. Slice onions thin and caramelize over medium heat for 30 to 40 minutes.

Combine horseradish, cream cheese, and salt and pepper.

Brush baguette slices with olive oil and toast in oven at 400°F for 10 to 12 minutes or until lightly golden.

To assemble, spread horseradish-cream cheese mixture on bread. Then top with roast beef followed by caramelized onions. Sprinkle with thyme.

Servings: 20 crostini

2 tablespoons butter

2 tablespoons olive oil

2 large onions, thinly sliced

2 to 3 tablespoons prepared horseradish

1 package (8 ounces) cream cheese

Salt and black pepper, to taste

1 baguette

1 pound thinly sliced deli roast beef (I like Boar's Head)

2 tablespoons thyme

Fall Feast

MENU

Beet Salad with Arugula, Oranges, Walnuts, Goat Cheese, and Sherry Vinaigrette

Pork Tenderloin with Figs and Balsamic Vinegar

Wild Rice Pilaf with Mushrooms

When the air turns crisp and the leaves start to fall, a pork tenderloin dinner immediately comes to mind. Start this meal with one of my favorite salad combos—beets and goat cheese. The sweetness of the beets and the slightly acidic, pithy taste of the goat cheese create a perfect flavor balance. Add the slight crunch of toasted walnuts, and now we're really talking. Not only is this dish delicious and full of flavor, but it's also packed with an antioxidant punch.

I like to serve this pork tenderloin for my guests every fall. The figs and balsamic vinegar go together marvelously to complement the pork. And don't worry if you've never used figs—they're low maintenance and pretty easy to find this time of year. However, if you can't find fresh figs, you can use dried. Soak them in chicken stock for a couple of minutes until they softens. The rice pilaf is a perfect accompaniment.

BEET SALAD

WITH ARUGULA, ORANGES, WALNUTS, GOAT CHEESE, AND SHERRY VINAIGRETTE

Servings: 4 to 6

For the dressing:

1 medium shallot, minced

2 tablespoons sherry vinegar

1 tablespoon fresh lemon juice

1 teaspoon Dijon mustard

½ cup extra-virgin olive oil

Fine sea salt and freshly ground black pepper, to taste

For the salad:

4 beets

¼ cup extra-virgin olive oil

Kosher salt and freshly ground black pepper, to taste

⅓ cup walnuts

1 bunch arugula, trimmed and torn

1 orange, peeled, segmented, and segments cut in half

4 ounces goat cheese (preferably Stickney Hill)

Directions

Stir shallot, vinegar, lemon juice, and Dijon in a small bowl. Gradually whisk in oil (or stir first 4 ingredients in a jar with a lid, add oil, screw on lid, and shake to combine). Season with salt and pepper. Cover and chill dressing in an airtight container for up to 1 week.

Preheat the oven to 400°F. Remove tops and the roots of the beets and peel each with a vegetable peeler. Cut the beets in half (large ones in quarters). Toss with olive oil and salt and pepper. Roast 35 to 40 minutes until beets are tender. Remove from oven and let cool.

While beets are cooling, heat a sauté pan to medium-high heat and add walnuts. Toast, stirring frequently, for about 5 minutes.

To assemble salad, lay a bed of arugula leaves on a serving plate. Slice beets thin and lay them overlapping on the arugula. Next, sprinkle walnuts, orange segments, and goat cheese over beets. Pour dressing over the top and serve.

PORK TENDERLOIN
WITH FIGS AND BALSAMIC VINEGAR

Servings: 4

1 pork tenderloin cut in ⅓-inch slices

Salt and black pepper for seasoning

1 cup flour

3 tablespoons olive oil, divided

¼ cup prosciutto

2 minced shallots

1 tablespoon minced thyme

3 tablespoons balsamic vinegar, divided

1 ½ cups canned low-salt chicken broth

6 mission figs, quartered

½ cup whipping cream

1 teaspoon Dijon mustard

1 tablespoon chopped parsley

Directions

Preheat oven to 200°F. Season pork with salt and pepper. Place flour in a bowl and dredge individual pork slices in flour. Heat 1 tablespoon oil in heavy large skillet over medium-high heat. Add as many pork slices as will fit without overcrowding and sauté until brown, about 2-3 minutes per side. Transfer pork to baking sheet. Add another tablespoon of oil to skillet. Repeat with remaining pork slices. Transfer pork to oven to keep warm.

Heat remaining tablespoon of oil in same skillet over medium-high heat. Add prosciutto and cook until crisp, 4 minutes. Add shallots and sauté until tender, about 2 minutes.

Add thyme and 2 tablespoons vinegar. Simmer until vinegar evaporates, scraping up any browned bits on bottom of skillet, about 1 minute.

Add chicken broth. Simmer until mixture is reduced by half, about 4 minutes. Add figs and whipping cream. Simmer until sauce thickens slightly, about 4 minutes. Add remaining tablespoon vinegar and 1 teaspoon mustard and any accumulated juices from pork.

Simmer until sauce thickens enough to coat spoon, about 4 to 5 minutes longer. Season sauce to taste with salt and pepper.

Arrange pork on plates. Spoon sauce over pork. Sprinkle with parsley and serve.

WILD RICE PILAF
WITH MUSHROOMS

Directions

Cook rice according to package instructions.

Heat 1 tablespoon of the butter in a large saucepan over medium heat. Add the onion and celery and season with salt and pepper. Cook, stirring often, until softened, approximately 5 minutes. Add mushrooms, season with salt and pepper, and cook, stirring occasionally, until mushrooms are browned, 6 to 8 minutes.

Add the wine and cook, scraping up the brown bits, until evaporated, 1 to 2 minutes.

Add the rice and cook, stirring, for 30 seconds.

Stir in parsley and season with salt and pepper.

Servings: 4 to 6

1 cup wild rice

2 tablespoons unsalted butter, divided

1 small onion, finely chopped

1 stalk celery, finely chopped

Kosher salt and black pepper, to taste

8 ounces baby bella mushrooms, chopped

¼ cup dry white wine

2 tablespoons chopped fresh parsley

Backyard Bonfire

MENU

Beer Cheese Soup

French Onion Soup

Everyone will appreciate a warm bowl of soup around the fire. Make sure you buy pretzel rolls or breadsticks to dunk in the beer cheese soup. It's the perfect combination.

French onion soup is so deliciously aromatic that you will attract visitors as you make it. There are always debates as to which version is best—red wine versus white wine, beef stock versus chicken stock. The following recipe is my favorite.

BEER CHEESE SOUP

Directions

In a Dutch oven, cook the bacon over moderate heat until the fat is rendered and the bacon is crisp. Using a slotted spoon, transfer the bacon onto paper towels.

Next, add the celery, onion, and carrots to the Dutch oven and cook over moderate heat, stirring, for about 5 minutes until softened.

Add the beer and chicken broth. Bring to a boil and reduce to a lively simmer for 12 minutes.

Next, add the Tabasco, cayenne, Dijon mustard, Worcestershire sauce, dry mustard, salt, and pepper. Reduce heat to low.

In a medium saucepan over medium-low heat, melt the butter. Add the flour and whisk over moderate heat, stirring, until lightly browned, about 2 minutes. Gradually stir in the milk, whisking until thickened, 2 to 3 minutes. Remove from the heat and add all the cheeses, stirring until incorporated. Add the cheese mixture to the Dutch oven. Mix well.

This soup can be refrigerated overnight. Rewarm it gently and thin it with additional broth.

Using an immersion blender or regular blender, process soup until smooth. Season with salt and pepper.

Serve with crumbled bacon on top.

Servings: 6 to 8

½ pound bacon, cut into ⅓-inch dice

2 celery ribs, diced

1 onion, diced

2 carrots, diced

1 bottle (12 ounces) lager or ale

2 cups chicken broth

½ teaspoon Tabasco sauce

¼ teaspoon cayenne

1 teaspoon Dijon mustard

2 teaspoons Worcestershire sauce

1 teaspoon dry mustard

1 teaspoon each salt and black pepper, plus extra for seasoning

½ stick (¼ cup) butter

⅓ cup flour

2 cups whole milk

4 ounces cream cheese

1 cup shredded Gouda cheese

2 cups shredded Cheddar Jack cheese

FRENCH ONION SOUP

Servings: 6 to 8

1 stick (½ cup) unsalted butter

4 onions, sliced

2 garlic cloves, chopped

2 bay leaves

2 sprigs fresh thyme

Kosher salt and freshly ground black pepper, to taste

1 cup red wine (about ⅓ bottle)

3 heaping tablespoons all-purpose flour

2 quarts beef broth

1 baguette, sliced

½ pound Gruyère cheese, grated

Directions

Melt the butter in a large pot over medium heat. Add the onions, garlic, bay leaves, thyme, salt, and pepper, and cook until the onions are very soft and caramelized, 35 to 45 minutes. Stir occasionally while cooking.

Add the wine, bring to a boil, reduce the heat, and simmer until the wine has evaporated and the onions are dry, about 5 minutes. Discard the bay leaves and thyme sprigs.

Dust the onions and garlic with the flour and give them a stir. Turn the heat down to medium-low so the flour doesn't burn, and cook for 10 minutes to cook out the raw flour taste. Now add the beef broth, bring the soup back to a simmer, and cook for 10 minutes. Season with salt and pepper.

When you're ready to eat, preheat the broiler. Arrange the baguette slices on a baking sheet in a single layer. Sprinkle the slices with the Gruyère, and broil until bubbly and golden brown, 3 to 5 minutes.

Ladle the soup into bowls and float several of the Gruyère croutons on top.

Elegant Dinner Party
(TO IMPRESS ANYONE)

MENU

Filet Mignon with Red Wine Sauce

Gratin Dauphinois

Roasted Asparagus

Bananas Foster

The recipes I've included here make up my go-to meal for an elegant dinner party. This meal of filet mignon drizzled with a stunning, rich red wine sauce, accompanied by a creamy potato gratin and roasted asparagus, and followed by bananas Foster, is restaurant-worthy. The gratin can be assembled and roasting in the oven by the time your guests arrive. This impressive meal is guaranteed to dazzle and delight.

Always bring meat to room temp for 30 minutes before cooking. This will help it sear and cook evenly.

FILET MIGNON

WITH RED WINE SAUCE

Directions

Season filets evenly with salt and pepper and Montreal steak seasoning.

Add 1 tablespoon each of butter and oil in large skillet over medium-high heat. Sear filets in skillet 2 to 3 minutes per side, until you get a nice crisp crust. Transfer beef to a foil-lined cookie sheet and place in oven. Roast at 425°F for 8 minutes for medium rare, or internal temp of 130°F. Remove from oven and tent steaks with aluminum foil to accumulate all the juices.

In the meantime, turn stovetop heat to medium-low and add the rest of the butter and canola oil to the skillet. Add garlic, shallots, and thyme and sauté until tender, about 3 minutes. Add flour; stir 1 minute. Add broth and wine. Bring to a boil and reduce sauce until it thickens to 1½ cups, stirring occasionally, about 12 minutes.

Return any collected juices to sauce in skillet; heat through, about 1 minute. Spoon sauce over the bottom of the plate and place the filet on top of sauce. Serve with Gratin Dauphinois and Roasted Asparagus (recipes follow).

Servings: 4

4 beef tenderloin filets (6 ounces each)

Salt and black pepper, to taste

2 tablespoons Montreal steak seasoning

2 tablespoons butter, divided

2 tablespoons canola oil, divided

4 large garlic cloves, chopped

3 large shallots, chopped (about ⅔ cup)

1 teaspoon dried thyme

1 tablespoon all-purpose flour

2 cups canned beef broth

2 cups dry red wine

GRATIN DAUPHINOIS

Servings: 6

1 garlic clove

2 pounds baking potatoes, peeled and sliced very thin (with a mandoline if possible)

1 cup freshly grated Gruyère cheese

1 cup heavy cream

Salt, to taste

Directions

Preheat oven to 350°F. Rub a baking dish with the garlic. Layer half of the potatoes in the dish, overlapping slightly. Sprinkle with half of the cheese and then half of the cream. Sprinkle with salt. Add another layer, using the rest of the ingredients. Bake uncovered until the gratin is crisp and golden on top, about 1 hour.

ROASTED ASPARAGUS

Servings: 6

1 bunch asparagus spears, trimmed

2 tablespoons olive oil

1 teaspoon sea salt

½ teaspoon ground black pepper

1 tablespoon lemon juice

Directions

Preheat oven to 425°F. Place the asparagus into a mixing bowl and drizzle with the olive oil. Toss to coat the spears. Sprinkle with salt and pepper. Arrange the asparagus on a baking sheet in a single layer. Bake in the preheated oven until just tender, 10 to 15 minutes depending on thickness. Drizzle lemon juice over spears and serve.

BANANAS FOSTER

Directions

Melt the butter in a heavy skillet over medium-high heat. Add the brown sugar and salt. Stir together and cook for 1 to 2 minutes. Pour in the cream and vanilla and stir to combine.

Add bananas to the pan. Stir in the rum, and then carefully use a long lighter to ignite it. Let the fire burn out; it'll only take about 30 seconds. (Be sure to have a lid handy in case you need to extinguish the flame.) You may also cook the mixture without flambéing it.

Spoon the mixture over a couple of scoops of vanilla ice cream and enjoy immediately.

Servings: 4

1 stick (½ cup) salted butter

1 cup packed dark brown sugar

¼ teaspoon salt

½ cup heavy cream

1 ½ teaspoons vanilla extract

4 bananas, peeled and cut in half crosswise, then lengthwise

½ cup dark rum

Vanilla ice cream

Cabin Cooking

MENU

On the Grill: Tandoori-ish Chicken Kebabs

In the Cooler: Summer Pasta Salad with Balsamic Lemon Basil Dressing

On the Dock: The Big Sammy

With our car packed to the brim, our family always heads to family and friends, cabins throughout the summer. When I want to bring something besides hot dogs and hamburgers, these smoky chicken kebabs fit the bill. You can marinate them ahead of time, then skewer and grill them whenever dinner rolls around. The spicy yogurt marinade is similar to the marinade for tandoori chicken. Yogurt is great for marinating because it helps the chicken stay moist and the kick of paprika gives it extra flavor. These kebabs are a perfect lake food and travel well in a cooler, and all the work done ahead means more time for me on my floatie.

The lemony summer flavors of the pasta salad make it a weekend-long hit at the lake. The Big Sammy is my choice for on-the-dock eating.

ON THE GRILL:
TANDOORI-ISH CHICKEN KEBABS

Directions

In a medium bowl, stir together yogurt, lemon juice, oil, ginger, salt, smoked paprika, garlic, black pepper, cumin, coriander, and cayenne pepper.

Add the chicken to the spices and stir to coat. Cover and refrigerate 2 to 4 hours.

Thread chicken tightly onto skewers.

Preheat grill for high heat.

Brush grill grate with oil and place skewers on grill. Grill for 15 to 20 minutes, occasionally turning kebabs to ensure even cooking.

Remove chicken from skewers onto a large platter. Add naan to platter and serve.

Servings: 6

1 cup plain yogurt

¼ cup freshly squeezed lemon juice

3 tablespoons extra-virgin olive oil

1 tablespoon fresh ginger, minced

1 tablespoon kosher salt

2 tablespoons smoked paprika

2 garlic cloves, minced

1 teaspoon black pepper

1 teaspoon ground cumin

1 teaspoon ground coriander

¼ teaspoon cayenne pepper

2 pounds boneless, skinless chicken breasts, cut into 1 ½-inch pieces

Naan (Indian flatbread)

IN THE COOLER:

SUMMER PASTA SALAD

WITH BALSAMIC LEMON BASIL DRESSING

Servings: 12

For the dressing:

1 garlic bulb

2 tablespoons plus ½ cup olive oil

Juice of 2 fresh lemons

¼ cup balsamic vinegar

¼ cup chopped fresh basil

1 teaspoon sea salt

1 teaspoon freshly ground cracked pepper

½ teaspoon red pepper flakes

2 tablespoons honey

1 teaspoon Dijon mustard

For the salad:

1 pound bowtie noodles

1 bag (8 ounces) spinach

1 medium seedless cucumber, peeled and diced

10 ounces cherry tomatoes, halved

1 cup chopped roasted red peppers

8 ounces crumbled feta cheese

8 ounces mozzarella cheese pearls, drained and cut in half

Salt and black pepper, to taste

Directions

Preheat oven to 400°F. Slice top ¼ of garlic bulb so garlic cloves are showing. Place on aluminum foil and drizzle with 2 tablespoons of olive oil. Wrap tightly in foil and roast garlic for 1 hour. Set aside to cool. When cool enough to handle, squeeze garlic cloves into a blender.

Mix all the remaining dressing ingredients together in the blender except the ½ cup olive oil. Then slowly drizzle in the oil mixture while the blender is running and blend completely.

Cook pasta according to package. Drain the pasta and rinse with cold water to completely cool the pasta.

In a large bowl, add pasta, spinach, cucumber, tomatoes, roasted red peppers, feta, and mozzarella and toss lightly. Season with salt and pepper.

Pour dressing over pasta salad and toss well to coat. Can be made 1 day ahead.

ON THE DOCK:
THE BIG SAMMY

Introduction

My good friend's husband makes a sandwich every night before bed. It drives her crazy. We used to go camping with them every summer when our kids were young. I would make this sandwich especially for him, and I used to giggle watching him sneak slices out of the cooler at midnight. Chris, this sandwich is for you.

Directions

Starting with the bottom half of the hoagie roll, layer all the ingredients except the dressing in the order listed. Put the dressing on the inside of the top half of the roll; poke the roll with a fork to help the dressing sink into the bread.

Wrap the sandwich in foil and put back in the bag the roll came in. Refrigerate about 1 hour. Sandwich can keep in the fridge for a couple of days.

As needed, slice 2-inch pieces off the sandwich, slicing through the foil so the sandwich doesn't fall apart.

Servings: 10 sandwich slices

1 long, wide hoagie roll, sliced lengthwise

Mustard

Mayonnaise

¾ pound shaved Boar's Head rosemary ham

¾ pound shaved Boar's Head turkey

About 30 slices pepperoni

14 pepperoncini rings (about ½ cup)

8 to 10 thin slices provolone cheese

8 to 10 thin slices Cojack cheese

1 head romaine, chopped

8 to 10 tomatoes, sliced very thinly

½ red onion, sliced very thinly

Italian seasoning, to taste

Salt and black pepper, to taste

Kraft Zesty Italian dressing

Feeding the Team

MENU

Stromboli

Roasted Garlic Meatballs

Basil Pesto Chicken

Blondies

Food makes kids happy. If you've ever hosted lots of kids, teenagers especially, you know it's amazing to watch them eat. Sixteen-year-old boys devour food like lions and go after whatever is on the last person's plate. This meal will satisfy all the kids in your life, young or old.

The little meatballs pack a flavor punch and are a kid favorite. I used to make them for my daughter's friend on her birthday. She would pop in ten at a time sitting at our kitchen island, and it always made me smile. These meatballs have an Italian twist and are so good they don't even need sauce.

Stromboli is like your favorite pizza toppings shoved into a deliciously soft-on-the-inside, crispy-on-the-outside shell. It is quick and easy to make. You can put anything in it, then roll it up and bake. Stromboli can also be made ahead and frozen up to a month in advance.

The basil pesto chicken is a great Italian dish, and with only a few ingredients, it's a cinch to make. The blondies are my mom's special recipe and one of my favorites.

ROASTED GARLIC MEATBALLS

Servings: 40 meatballs

Olive oil

3 bulbs of garlic, root ends cut off

2 shallots, minced

2 teaspoons fresh minced thyme

1 teaspoon fresh minced basil

12 ounces ground beef

12 ounces ground pork

1 egg

1 ¼ cup unseasoned bread crumbs

¾ cup freshly grated Parmigiano-Reggiano cheese

⅛ cup milk

Salt and freshly ground black pepper

½ cup flour

Directions

Cut off the heads of garlic, drizzle olive oil over garlic bulbs and wrap with aluminum foil. Bake at 400°F until soft, about 1 hour. Cool garlic and squeeze the garlic paste out of the skin into a small bowl. Set aside.

Sauté shallots in 1 teaspoon of olive oil on medium-low heat until tender, 5 to 7 minutes. Cool.

Combine all ingredients but flour and mix with your hands until incorporated. Shape into balls, and roll in flour to lightly coat.

Fry in olive oil until lightly browned, 7 to 10 minutes, using forks to roll them around. Remove to lined cookie sheet.

Serve with favorite pasta sauce if desired.

STROMBOLI

Servings: 4 to 6

1 loaf pizza dough (Trader Joe's)

1 container (10 ounces) pizza sauce (Trader Joe's)

1 package (6 ounces) sliced pepperoni (Trader Joe's)

2 ounces sliced provolone cheese

½ cup shredded mozzarella cheese

¼ cup grated Parmesan cheese

1 teaspoon Italian seasoning

1 egg yolk, lightly beaten

Directions

Preheat oven to 375°F.

Roll out pizza dough into a rectangular shape. Spread desired amount of pizza sauce over the dough, leaving a 2-inch border.

Arrange pepperoni and provolone cheese over the sauce. Sprinkle with the mozzarella cheese, Parmesan cheese, and Italian seasoning. (Or use any ingredients you like; these are just suggested fillings.)

Roll up the dough rectangle like a jelly roll, beginning with one of the long sides (much like rolling cinnamon rolls). When finished rolling, seal the seam and ends by pinching the dough closed with your fingers. Line a cookie sheet with aluminum foil or parchment paper that has been sprayed with a nonstick cooking spray. Place seam-side-down on sheet. Brush with egg yolk and sprinkle with additional Italian seasoning.

Bake at 375°F for 20 to 30 minutes or until golden brown. Let stand for 5 minutes before slicing.

If you're making this ahead, prepare the stromboli as directed except for egg wash. Cover with plastic wrap and aluminum foil. Freeze for up to a month.

BASIL PESTO CHICKEN

Servings: 4 to 6

2 packages (14 ounces each) chicken tenders

Salt, black pepper, and cayenne pepper, to taste

Cooking spray

1 cup basil pesto

½ cup chicken broth

4 ounces cream cheese

1 cup grated mozzarella cheese

3 Roma tomatoes, sliced

Directions

Preheat oven to 350°F.

Season the chicken with salt, pepper, and cayenne pepper as desired.

Spray a 9-inch by 12-inch baking dish with nonstick spray. Lay chicken tenders over the bottom.

Heat a large skillet over medium heat. Add the pesto and chicken broth to the skillet. Stir to combine and allow it to come to a simmer. Add the cream cheese in chunks and whisk it into the hot liquid until a smooth sauce forms.

Pour the pesto mixture over the chicken tenders and top with mozzarella cheese. Cover the baking dish with aluminum foil and bake the chicken 20 minutes. Remove the foil and top with Roma tomatoes. Put dish back into the oven without foil and cook 5 to 10 minutes more, just until the cheese is melted. Serve hot.

BLONDIES

Servings: 24 bars

- Cooking spray
- 3 cups cake flour
- 1 tablespoon baking powder
- ¾ teaspoon salt
- ¾ pound unsalted butter
- 3 cups packed light brown sugar
- 3 large eggs
- 1 tablespoon vanilla extract

Directions

Adjust oven rack to lowest position; heat to 325°F. Spray a 9-inch by 13-inch baking pan with vegetable cooking spray. Fit a 12-inch by 18-inch piece of heavy-duty foil into the pan so that you can use the foil overhang as a handle to pull the baked blondies from the pan. Coat the foil with cooking spray.

Whisk flour, baking powder, and salt in a small bowl. Then heat butter and brown sugar in a large pan until bubbling hot. Whisk eggs and vanilla in a large bowl. Slowly whisk hot sugar mixture, then dry ingredients, into eggs.

Scrape batter into prepared pan, and then bake until blondies are just set, about 45 minutes. Remove from oven and let cool for 5 minutes. Pull blondies from the pan using foil handles and set on a wire rack. Cool completely before cutting into 24 pieces.

Provence Dinner Party

(YACHT NOT INCLUDED)

MENU

Caramelized Onion, Gorgonzola, and Pecan Pizzette

Pan-Roasted Halibut with Pancetta, Capers, and Lemon White Wine Sauce

Provençal Roasted Tomatoes

The summer I was studying international management in graduate school, I finagled my way to Nice, France. I had a language requirement to fulfill, and I convinced my professor (and my dad) that I would learn so much more studying in Nice than if I were sitting in a classroom for a semester. Surrounded by fluent French-speaking European students, I had my work cut out for me. Truth be told, I wasn't very good at speaking French, but I was *really good* at exploring the Mediterranean coast with my French bob and summer dresses. Most nights, I would gallivant down the promenade, sightseeing, exploring, and hanging out at cafés, trying the local fare. I just couldn't get enough of the Mediterranean cuisine.

You could go all out and make these dishes together for a dinner party, or you could enjoy any of them on their own. The caramelized onion pizzette is a favorite at all parties—the perfect punch of savory and sweet. Sliced into little bites, it will be a perfect start to your dinner party.

The fish is full of flavor, with a trifecta of tomatoes, olives, and capers. It's light and satisfying. Just make sure you have a loaf of crusty French bread to scoop up every last drop of sauce. The Provençal Roasted Tomatoes are a flavorful, easy side dish to accompany the fish.

CARAMELIZED ONION, GORGONZOLA, AND PECAN PIZZETTE

Directions

Sauté onions in butter over medium-high heat for 10 minutes. Turn heat down to medium and sauté until onions are caramelized, approximately 10-15 minutes more.

Stir in brown sugar, salt, and pepper.

Once mixture is gooey, add pecans and stir to coat.

Cool mixture to room temperature.

Spread mixture evenly on pizza crust, all the way to the edges.

Sprinkle Gorgonzola evenly on top. Bake at 350°F for 20 to 25 minutes until cheese sets. Cut into squares and serve at room temperature.

Servings: 6 to 8

1 red onion, sliced thin

½ stick (¼ cup) unsalted butter

½ cup brown sugar

2 teaspoons sea salt

¾ tablespoons freshly ground black pepper

½ cup pecan pieces

1 thin Boboli pizza crust

½ cup crumbled Gorgonzola cheese

PAN-ROASTED HALIBUT

WITH PANCETTA, CAPERS, AND LEMON WHITE WINE SAUCE

Servings: 4

- 4 (6-ounce) halibut fillets
- Salt and freshly ground black pepper, to taste
- 4 tablespoons butter, divided
- 2 tablespoons extra-virgin olive oil, divided
- 2 ounces pancetta, sliced
- 1 garlic clove, minced
- ¾ cup dry white wine
- 2 tablespoons lemon juice
- 3 tablespoons capers
- 1 tablespoon herbes de Provence

Directions

Sprinkle Halibut fillets with salt and pepper on both sides. Heat a large skillet over medium-high heat. Add 2 tablespoons each butter and olive oil. Place Halibut filets in pan and cook 3-4 minutes per side until lightly browned. Transfer them to a plate and cover with foil.

Next, add pancetta and cook until crisp, 3-4 minutes. Add garlic and cook 30 seconds. Pour in wine, lemon juice, capers, and herbes de Provence and the remaining two tablespoons of butter. Bring to a high simmer and reduce by a third, approximately 3-4 minutes.

Transfer fish to plates and pour sauce over fish. Serve with roasted tomatoes.

PROVENÇAL ROASTED TOMATOES

Servings: 4 to 6

3 cups halved cherry tomatoes

2 teaspoons salt, divided

1 teaspoon black pepper, divided

4 tablespoons olive oil, divided

¼ cup finely chopped shallots

2 tablespoons chopped parsley

1 tablespoon minced thyme

2 garlic cloves, minced

Pinch of sugar

2 tablespoons balsamic vinegar

Directions

Preheat oven to 400°F. Place tomatoes in a single layer on a sheet pan and toss with 1 teaspoon salt, ½ teaspoon pepper, and 1 tablespoon olive oil.

In small bowl, mix together shallots, parsley, thyme, garlic, sugar, and remaining salt and pepper. Spread over tomatoes. Drizzle remaining oil and balsamic vinegar. Bake for 15 to 20 minutes.

Serve immediately alongside the fish or let cool and store in airtight container for up to a week.

Cinco de Mayo Celebration

MENU

Guacamole

Corn Pudding

Braised Beef Tacos with Jalapeño Slaw and Street Sauce

Mexican food is the perfect party food, so put on your sombreros and shake your maracas because you will love every bite of this feast. One of the best parts is that the shredded beef tacos can be made in advance in a slow cooker, so you can get a jump start on your party planning. The jalapeño slaw and street sauce complete these food-truck–worthy tacos, giving you a great meal for summer parties and weekend gatherings. The roasted garlic and green Tabasco make this guacamole our favorite, and the side dish of corn pudding is major comfort food.

Buy avocados that are firm to touch but give a little. You can use them immediately.

GUACAMOLE

Servings: 8 to 10

- 1 head garlic
- 1 tablespoon olive oil
- 4 whole avocados
- Juice of ½ lime
- Kosher salt, to taste
- 10 drops Tabasco Green Pepper Sauce
- 1 tablespoon Worcestershire sauce
- Tortilla chips

Directions

Cut the top off a head of garlic. Drizzle with olive oil and wrap in foil. Bake for 1 hour at 400°F until garlic is soft. Peel avocados, remove pits, and place avocados in bowl. Squeeze roasted garlic out of papery skins and into bowl. Mash together. Add lime juice, salt, green pepper sauce, and Worcestershire sauce. Adjust seasoning to taste. Serve with tortilla chips.

CORN PUDDING

Servings: 8 to 10

- 4 eggs
- 1 box Jiffy corn bread mix
- 1 can (15 ounces) creamed corn
- ½ cup canola oil
- ½ teaspoon garlic salt
- ½ cup grated cheddar cheese

Directions

Preheat oven to 350°F. Beat eggs and then mix with remaining ingredients. Pour into a greased 4-quart casserole. Sprinkle with cheese and bake for 45 to 60 minutes, uncovered, until pudding is set.

BRAISED BEEF TACOS
WITH JALAPEÑO SLAW AND STREET SAUCE

Servings: 8 to 10

For the slaw:

Juice of 1 lime

2 jalapeño peppers, stemmed, seeded, and chopped fine

1 bag (14 ounces) coleslaw mix

¼ cup cilantro, chopped

½ cup white wine vinegar

1 tablespoon kosher salt

1 teaspoon sugar

For the sauce:

½ cup mayonnaise

2 tablespoons rice wine vinegar

1 tablespoon horseradish

1 teaspoon Cholula hot sauce

1 tablespoon chopped cilantro

For taco assembly:

Corn and flour tortillas

Queso fresco

Salsa

For the beef:

2 pounds beef round

1 tablespoon kosher salt

1 tablespoon ground black pepper

2 cloves garlic, smashed

1 large onion, sliced

1 can (28 ounces) crushed tomatoes (preferably San Marzano brand)

1 tablespoon ancho chili powder

1 tablespoon cayenne pepper

1 tablespoon ground cumin

3 bay leaves

Directions

Put all the beef ingredients in a slow cooker and cook on low for 8 to 9 hours or on high for 6 to 7 hours. When cooked through, take out meat and shred. Put shredded meat back in juices. Adjust seasonings and keep warm in slow cooker until ready to serve.

To make the slaw, combine the lime juice, jalapeños, coleslaw mix, and cilantro in a large bowl. Add the vinegar and toss to coat evenly, then add the salt and sugar. Mix well, then cover and refrigerate. Can be made up to 2 days ahead.

To make the sauce, mix all sauce ingredients together and refrigerate. Can be made up to 2 days ahead.

To assemble the tacos, spread the sauce on a tortilla, then top with shredded beef, slaw, cheese, salsa, and any other fixings of your choosing.

For the beef, I typically buy a double pack of beef top round roast at Costco.

For the slaw, use fewer jalapeños if you like less heat.

I like to double the sauce recipe because I use it on everything.

Potluck

(YEP, ANOTHER ONE)

MENU

Chicken Chili

Corn Bread with Mascarpone Honey Spread

Homemade Fritos

This "award-winning" chicken chili is my husband's recipe. He uses Ro-Tel tomatoes and a craft beer of your choosing. I've made it countless times for potlucks and hosting informal gatherings. It never disappoints, and I always get requests for the recipe.

Serving corn bread with your chili is a way to go the extra mile for your guests. This super moist bread slathered with a honey-infused mascarpone cheese spread will disappear as fast as you can set the plate down. Homemade Fritos are fun and easy to make, adding that special touch to your next Potluck gathering.

CHICKEN CHILI

Servings: 6

- 1 pound boneless, skinless chicken breast, cubed
- 2 tablespoons olive oil, divided
- 1 onion, chopped
- 1 packet chili seasoning
- 1 can (14.5 ounces) Ro-Tel tomatoes
- 1 can (28 ounces) plus 1 can (15 ounces) tomato sauce
- 1 can black beans (not drained)
- 1 can chili beans (not drained)
- 1 can kidney beans (not drained)
- 1 bottle (12 ounces) of your favorite beer (I use Surly Furious)

Directions

Sauté the chicken in a Dutch oven with 1 tablespoon olive oil over medium-high heat until cooked through, approximately 8 to 10 minutes. Transfer chicken to a plate. Pour the remaining tablespoon of olive oil into the Dutch oven, add onion, and cook until soft, 5 to 10 minutes.

Add chili seasoning and mix. Add tomatoes, tomato sauce, beans, and beer.

Simmer for 30 to 45 minutes to let flavors blend.

Serve with cheese, sour cream, green onions, and homemade corn chips (recipe follows).

CORN BREAD
WITH MASCARPONE HONEY SPREAD

Servings: 4 to 6

- 1 cup cornmeal
- 1 cup all-purpose flour
- ⅓ cup sugar
- 2 teaspoons baking powder
- ½ teaspoon salt, plus a pinch
- 2 eggs
- 1 stick (½ cup) butter, melted
- 1 cup milk
- ½ cup mascarpone cheese
- 2 tablespoons honey

Directions

Preheat oven to 400°F. Grease an 8- or 9-inch square baking pan and set aside.

In a large bowl, mix together cornmeal, flour, sugar, baking powder, and salt. Add eggs, butter, and milk; stir gently to combine.

Pour batter into baking pan, and bake for 15 to 20 minutes, or until a toothpick inserted into the corn bread comes out clean.

Blend mascarpone cheese and honey with a mixer for 1 to 2 minutes until incorporated. Add a pinch of salt and serve with corn bread.

HOMEMADE FRITOS

Servings: 6 to 8

½ cup canola oil

1 teaspoon sea salt

2 teaspoons chili powder

1 teaspoon cumin

1 teaspoon onion powder

1 teaspoon garlic powder

6 yellow corn tortillas

Directions

Heat canola oil in a large skillet over medium-high heat.

Add all spices and seasonings to a large bowl and whisk until well combined. Set aside.

Using a knife or pizza cutter, cut your tortillas into equal strips.

Fry strips in small batches for 30 seconds. Remove with a slotted spoon.

Once removed, immediately add tortilla strips to the seasoning mix and toss to coat.

Transfer to a serving bowl to shake off excess seasoning.

Serve with chicken chili.

It's All about the Brunch

MENU

Bourbon-Soaked Cherry Brie Bites

Mediterranean Quiche

Ham, Swiss, Cheddar, and Parmesan Strata

This menu is perfect for hosting a baby shower, a bridal shower, or a brunch for any occasion. It will have your guests lingering long after brunch is over.

The savory Brie bites are a great starter for when your guests arrive. The quiche is vegetarian and packs tons of flavor with sun-dried tomatoes, basil, and Gruyère.

You don't often see strata on brunch menus, but in my opinion, it's just about the best way to prepare baked eggs, and it's so easy to make. The base of the strata is bread cubes left to soak in a custardy egg mixture. The bread makes the strata light and fluffy; it's a lot like a savory bread pudding that you get to eat for breakfast. This is a basic recipe, so feel free to add broccoli, asparagus, mushrooms, peppers—really, whatever you like. You can use any kind of bread, but I think the onion rolls are the best.

BOURBON-SOAKED CHERRY BRIE BITES

Servings: 24

- 1 cup dried, tart cherries
- ½ cup bourbon (your favorite kind)
- 2 tablespoons light corn syrup
- 1 package (17.5 ounces) puff pastry dough
- 1 pound Brie cheese, cut into ½-inch cubes
- Freshly ground black pepper, to taste
- 2 eggs, beaten

Directions

Soak cherries in bourbon overnight.

Place Brie cubes on a parchment-lined cookie sheet and refrigerate until assembly.

Cook cherry-bourbon mixture in a saucepan on medium-low heat until fruit softens, 10 to 15 minutes, then add corn syrup and mix well. Using a food processor or blender, purée the mixture, then chill in refrigerator until cool.

Heat oven to 425°F.

Roll out puff pastry thinly and cut into 2 ½-inch squares. Dollop Brie and cherry mixture in the middle of each square. Season with pepper, then fold dough so all corners are sealed together. Shape into rounds with the seam on the bottom.

Spray a baking sheet with nonstick cooking spray and place pastries on tray. Brush each pastry with egg.

Bake for 10 to 15 minutes or until golden brown.

Serve immediately.

MEDITERRANEAN QUICHE

Servings: 8

2 prepared 9-inch piecrusts

2 tablespoons unsalted butter

1 medium onion, diced

1 red bell pepper, diced

8 ounces mushrooms, chopped

1 medium zucchini, peeled and chopped

2 teaspoons salt, divided

2 teaspoons ground black pepper, divided

4 ounces oil-packed sun-dried tomatoes, drained and chopped

2 tablespoons fresh basil, chopped

1 tablespoon fresh thyme, chopped

½ teaspoon red pepper flakes

6 ounces feta cheese, crumbled

8 large eggs

2 cups whole milk

2 cups grated white cheddar cheese

Directions

Preheat the oven to 375°F. Prepare 2 pie plates with the piecrusts. Crimp edges and set aside.

Melt the butter in a large skillet over medium-high heat. Add the onion and red pepper and cook for 5 minutes. Add the mushrooms and zucchini, stirring until liquid is absorbed, about 10 minutes. Season with ½ teaspoon salt and ½ teaspoon pepper.

Add the tomatoes, basil, thyme, and red pepper flakes. Season with ½ teaspoon salt and ½ teaspoon pepper. Cook, stirring, for 1 minute. Remove skillet from the heat and stir in feta cheese. Let the mixture cool.

After mixture has cooled, spoon into the prepared piecrusts, spreading it out evenly.

In a bowl, beat the eggs and milk together. Add 1 cup of white cheddar and 1 teaspoon each salt and pepper.

Divide the egg mixture evenly into both piecrusts. Sprinkle remaining cheese on top of quiches. Bake for 45 to 50 minutes until set. Remove from the oven and let cool for 10 minutes before serving.

HAM, SWISS, CHEDDAR, AND PARMESAN STRATA

Servings: 8 to 10

- 14 ounces onion rolls, chopped in 1-inch cubes
- ½ pound deli ham, chopped
- 1 cup shredded Swiss cheese
- 1 cup shredded cheddar cheese
- ½ cup shredded Parmigiano-Reggiano cheese
- 8 eggs
- 2 teaspoons Dijon mustard
- 3 cups 2 percent milk
- 1 teaspoon each salt and black pepper

Directions

Preheat oven to 375°F. Butter a 9-inch by 11-inch baking dish. Place cubed rolls in pan. Top with ham and cheeses.

Combine eggs, mustard, milk, salt, and pepper; whisk well. Pour over rolls, ham, and cheese.

Bake 30 to 45 minutes, until set and puffed. Let cool 10 minutes and serve.

Fourth of July
(AND ANYTIME YOU WANT TO BE A ROCK STAR AT THE GRILL)

MENU

Tonja's Table Burgers with Special Sauce

Best Barbecue Chicken

Charred Corn Salad with Cotija and Buttermilk

Watermelon, Feta, Basil, and Mint Salad

Here are my favorite burger and barbecue chicken recipes for celebrating the Fourth of July, along with my go-to summer salads. You cannot go wrong celebrating with this menu.

When you form the burger patties, get them as thin as you can by sandwiching the hamburger meat between 2 sheets of wax or parchment paper on a cookie sheet. Freeze them for at least an hour. If you want a healthier version, use ground turkey.

BEST BARBECUE CHICKEN

Serves: 4 to 6

For the brine:

2 quarts water

2 tablespoons kosher salt

¼ cup brown sugar

2 garlic cloves, smashed with the side of a large knife

4 sprigs fresh thyme

For the chicken:

3 skin-on, bone-in chicken breasts

6 skin-on, bone-in chicken thighs

Famous Dave's Rich & Sassy barbecue sauce

Directions

For the brine, combine the water, salt, sugar, garlic, and thyme in a large container. Add the chicken, cover, and refrigerate at least 4 hours.

Preheat grill to medium-high heat. Spray grill with nonstick spray and clean the hot grates, making a nonstick surface.

Take the chicken out of the brine, place on cookie sheet, and pat it dry on paper towels. Place chicken breasts on grill, bone side down. After 5 minutes add chicken thighs, bone side down. Cook 15 minutes from the time you put the chicken breasts on the grill. Turn chicken over and cook for an additional 10 minutes. Add sauce to 1 side and cook for 3 minutes. Flip over (skin side should be up), add sauce, and cook an additional 3 minutes.

Transfer to a platter and serve.

TONJA'S TABLE BURGERS
WITH SPECIAL SAUCE

Servings: 4 to 6

For the special sauce:

½ cup mayonnaise

⅓ cup ketchup

2 tablespoons finely chopped pickles

¼ teaspoon hot sauce

Kosher salt and freshly ground black pepper, to taste

For the burgers:

1 pound ground beef or ground turkey

1 tablespoon Montreal steak seasoning

Hamburger buns

Shredded lettuce

1 tablespoon ketchup

1 tablespoon yellow mustard

1 tablespoon Worcestershire sauce

Directions

Mix all ingredients for special sauce together and refrigerate. Make up to 2 days ahead.

Mix all ingredients for burgers together in a mixing bowl.

Make burger patties, transfer to a cookie sheet and freeze until ready to grill. When ready to grill, take burgers out and grill over medium-high heat 4 to 5 minutes a side until cooked through. Assemble the burgers and buns, and top with special sauce.

Tips for Grilling

Use the right equipment, including:

- *Spray bottle for flare-ups*
- *Brush for basting*
- *Metal tongs for flipping and moving things around on the grill.*

1. Always have a clean oiled grill. Its helps reduce sticking food and flare-ups.
2. Scrub your grill clean with a grill brush. Then with a brush,rub the entire grate with cooking oil.
3. Bring ingredients to room temperature for about 30 minutes before putting them on the grill.
4. Use a thermometer and take the guesswork out of cooking meats on the grill.
5. Marinate your meat for a juicer flavor. Most marinades take a few hours to do the trick. Plan ahead.
6. Prevent flare-ups by keeping a spray bottle filled with water at the grill, ready to use.
7. Flip once and limit handling items on the grill. Grill completely on 1 side before flipping, and then cook completely on the other side. This helps meat hold on to its juices.
8. Use a grill basket for foods that might fall through grill rack (vegetables, fish, fruits).
9. Let food rest and tent with foil to keep warm. I usually allow approximately 10 minutes before cutting meat. This allows the juices to absorb back into meat.

WATERMELON, FETA, BASIL, AND MINT SALAD

Directions

Combine watermelon with lime juice and let marinate for 30 minutes.

Arrange arugula over large platter. Scatter watermelon, feta, red onion, basil, and mint on top. Sprinkle with salt and pepper. Drizzle with olive oil and balsamic glaze.

Serve immediately.

Balsamic vinegar glaze can be found in the vinegar section at many supermarkets.

Servings: 6 to 8

8 cups cubed seedless watermelon

¼ cup fresh lime juice

4 cups baby arugula

1 cup crumbled feta cheese

¼ cup finely chopped red onion

¼ cup chopped fresh basil

¼ cup chopped fresh mint

1 teaspoon salt

½ teaspoon black pepper

2 tablespoons extra-virgin olive oil

2 tablespoons balsamic glaze

CHARRED CORN SALAD
WITH COTIJA AND BUTTERMILK

Servings: 6 to 8

For the dressing:

⅔ cup buttermilk

¼ cup mayonnaise

1 tablespoon cider vinegar

1 tablespoon snipped fresh chives

1 teaspoon Dijon mustard

1 teaspoon sugar

½ teaspoon hot red pepper sauce

For the salad:

8 ears fresh corn, husked

1 tablespoon olive oil, plus extra for brushing

1 bunch scallions, sliced

½ cup diced orange bell pepper

½ cup diced red bell pepper

½ cup diced yellow bell pepper

¾ teaspoon kosher salt

¾ teaspoon black pepper

1 cup crumbled Cotija cheese

½ cup chopped parsley

Directions

Whisk dressing ingredients in a bowl until blended. Refrigerate until meal is ready to serve.

Heat grill to medium-high heat. Lightly coat corn with olive oil. Grill corn 10 to 15 minutes, turning several times, until lightly charred and tender. Cut kernels from cobs into a medium bowl.

In the meantime, add 1 tablespoon olive oil to a large sauté pan over medium-high heat. Add scallions and peppers and sauté until tender, 5 to 8 minutes. Remove from heat and set aside to cool slightly.

Add cooled pepper mixture to the corn. Season with salt and pepper. Sprinkle cheese and parsley over the top. Mix all together and serve with dressing.

Essential Holiday Dinner

MENU

Smoked Trout Dip

Beef Tenderloin Bar

Red Pepper Aioli

Horseradish Sauce

Basil Curry Mayonnaise

Caramelized Onions

Roasted Fingerling Potatoes

Mixed Greens with Goat Cheese and Walnut Vinaigrette

We are a pretty casual bunch in our home during the holidays, but we love good food, and we love to treat our guests while they're here. To me nothing beats a succulent beef tenderloin for these holiday feasts. With such a great cut of meat, it's really easy to prepare, and the sauces give this meal an extra-special touch.

You can do all of this ahead of time and set it out buffet-style so everyone can keep coming back for more. I also like to have some caramelized onions to add a sweet and savory note. You can make these ahead of time, too. Pick and choose from the menu below so your holiday entertaining can be enjoyable and relaxing.

SMOKED TROUT DIP

Directions

Discard the skin, and flake the trout fillets. Purée the cream cheese and sour cream in a food processor. Add the fish and pulse a few times to break it up but not purée it. Transfer to a bowl and stir in the shallot, dill, and lemon juice. Salt and pepper to taste. Refrigerate until firm, about 1 hour. Serve with endive and favorite crackers.

Servings: 12

1 boneless smoked trout (about 8 ounces)

½ cup cream cheese, softened

½ cup sour cream

1 tablespoon minced shallot

1 tablespoon minced dill

Juice of ½ lemon

Salt and pepper, to taste

Crackers

BEEF TENDERLOIN BAR

Servings: 12

- 5 pounds beef tenderloin, trimmed
- Kosher salt
- Freshly ground black pepper
- Montreal steak seasoning
- Olive oil

Directions

Remove the beef from the refrigerator 30 minutes before roasting and let it come to room temperature. Preheat oven to 425°F.

Rub salt, pepper, and Montreal steak seasoning on the tenderloin. Then slather it with olive oil.

Put the roast on a rimmed baking sheet or in a shallow roasting pan. Roast until an instant-read thermometer inserted in the center reads 120°F for rare, 125°F to 130°F for medium-rare, or 135°F for medium (25 to 45 minutes for a 5-pound roast or 20 to 30 minutes for a 2 ½-pound roast).

Cover tenderloin loosely with foil, and let it rest for 10 to 15 minutes before carving. The temp will continue to rise 5 to 10 degrees out of the oven, and the juices will have time to accumulate.

Slice thin and serve on a platter with red pepper aioli, horseradish sauce, basil curry mayonnaise, caramelized onions, and your favorite mini rolls or buns (recipes follow).

RED PEPPER AIOLI

Servings: 8 to 10

- 1 ⅓ cups jarred roasted red bell peppers, drained well and patted dry
- 1 cup mayonnaise
- 2 teaspoons sambal oelek chili paste
- Salt and freshly ground black pepper, to taste

Directions

Blend the bell peppers, mayonnaise, and chili paste in a food processor until smooth and creamy. Season with salt and pepper. Cover and refrigerate.

HORSERADISH SAUCE

Servings: 10 to 12

- 2 cups sour cream
- ¼ cup prepared horseradish
- 1 tablespoon minced chives
- 1 teaspoon champagne or white wine vinegar
- 1 teaspoon salt, plus extra for seasoning
- Dash hot red pepper sauce
- Black pepper, to taste

Directions

In a bowl, combine all the ingredients and blend well. Season to taste with salt and pepper. Cover and refrigerate.

BASIL CURRY MAYONNAISE

Servings: 10 to 12

1 cup mayonnaise

¼ cup mascarpone cheese, room temperature

⅓ cup finely chopped fresh basil leaves

1 tablespoon curry powder

1 teaspoon smoked paprika

Kosher salt and freshly ground black pepper, to taste

Directions

In a small bowl, whisk together the mayonnaise, mascarpone cheese, basil, curry powder, and paprika until smooth. Season with salt and pepper. Cover and refrigerate.

CARAMELIZED ONIONS

Servings: 10 to 12

2 tablespoons butter

2 tablespoons olive oil

2 medium yellow onions, halved and sliced paper thin (about 4 cups)

Kosher salt

Freshly ground black pepper

Directions

Melt the butter and oil in a large frying pan over medium-high heat until foaming.

Add the onions and let them cook about 5 minutes, stirring occasionally. Turn down heat to medium-low and continue stirring occasionally until onions are deep golden brown and caramelized, 35 to 45 minutes.

Season well with salt and pepper, remove from the pan, and let cool.

ROASTED FINGERLING POTATOES

Servings: 6 to 8

20 fingerling potatoes, washed and scrubbed, halved lengthwise

⅓ cup extra-virgin olive oil, plus 2 tablespoons

2 tablespoons minced fresh thyme

Sea salt and freshly ground black pepper, to taste

Directions

Preheat the oven to 450°F.

In a large mixing bowl, toss the potatoes with olive oil, thyme, and a generous seasoning of salt and pepper. Coat a small roasting pan with the remaining olive oil and put the potatoes in the pan, cut side down.

Bake for 30-35 minutes, until the potatoes are tender on the inside and golden on the outside.

Let the potatoes cool slightly and then arrange on a serving platter.

MIXED GREENS
WITH GOAT CHEESE AND WALNUT VINAIGRETTE

Servings: 4

For the dressing:

¼ cup olive oil

2 tablespoons walnut oil

3 tablespoons tarragon vinegar

2 garlic cloves, minced

For the salad:

16 ounces mixed greens

½ pint cherry tomatoes, halved

8 ounces goat cheese, crumbled

1 cup chopped walnuts

Directions

To make the dressing, mix together the olive oil, walnut oil, vinegar, and garlic and season well with salt and pepper.

To make the salad, toss the greens, goat cheese, tomatoes, and toasted walnuts together in a bowl. Toss with dressing and serve.

The Perfect Charcuterie Platter

Here is the most delicious way to have dinner when you don't feel like cooking: a charcuterie, cheese, crackers, and fruit platter. One platter, four food groups, and a glass of rosé—no utensils needed.

When selecting the cheese, I like to include a variety of textures and flavors. Most cheese belongs to one of four basic categories: aged, soft, firm, or blue. For a good variety, choose at least one from each group.

You can find everything on my platter at Trader Joe's—reasonably priced and delicious.

Assemble and enjoy.

Servings: 10-12

Cheese:

Sharp cheddar

Honey goat cheese

Mini Basque

Stilton

Meats:

Prosciutto

Genoa salami

Bresaola

Fruit:

Champagne grapes

Bartlett pear

Green apple

Crackers:

Parmesan crisps

Fig and olive crisps

Nuts:

Candied pecans

JOEL GOTT
Sauvignon Blanc
2014

Two

WEEKEND COOKING

Weekend cooking should be all about food that's fun and inviting. We eat out plenty, but I think the real fun happens in the kitchen. Weekend cooking can be low and slow, or it can be impromptu. People *love* impromptu gatherings. A spontaneous party doesn't give anyone enough time to be flawless, so no one expects perfection. And perfection is not the point anyway; connection is. It's harder to connect when we're trying to be perfect instead of being ourselves.

I remember a weekend years ago when several of the neighborhood families were having a big garage sale. We were on our last day, and the kids all wanted a dinner party. We wrangled up whatever we could find in our house and had an eclectic mix of everything. Everyone helped in the kitchen, people came and went, and the atmosphere was relaxed and fun. I remember thinking, "We need to find more ways to open up our homes like this and not be so buttoned up."

We all occasionally have planned weekend guests, too, and no-pressure entertaining is the best kind. That's why I like menus that can be made ahead, even if there is a little extra work involved. When something is cooked low and slow, it tastes amazing. I love having a great pasta sauce made ahead of time, so all I have to do is boil noodles, or making a slow-roasted cut of meat that builds flavor over time. And a really good steak sauce or a thoughtfully crafted made-ahead condiment spread can give any dish a dollop of goodness guests will enjoy.

For weekend cooking, I also think family-style platters make everything more informal and fun. I love when people have to pass things around and get a little messy. Messy is good. Lay everything out on big platters and have your guests assemble their own plates. This way, they create their own meals just the way they like.

Impromptu Gatherings

MENU

Tomato Bruschetta

Green Olive and Cream Cheese Toasts

Jalapeño and Roasted Red Pepper Crostini

With a few pantry ingredients always on hand, impromptu gatherings can be fun. Who doesn't love to be invited on a whim? No one has time to contemplate hairdos, outfits, or smudges on refrigerators. Have people over because you like them more than you like a spotless house.

TOMATO BRUSCHETTA

Servings: 20 pieces

6 plum tomatoes, chopped

1 to 2 cloves garlic, minced

3 to 4 tablespoons chopped basil

3 tablespoons extra-virgin olive oil, plus extra for brushing

1 to 2 tablespoons good-quality balsamic vinegar

Salt and pepper, to taste

1 French baguette

Parmigiano-Reggiano cheese

Directions

Mix tomato, garlic, basil, olive oil, and vinegar together in a bowl. Season with salt and pepper and set aside, unrefrigerated, to marinate until ready to serve. Drain the mixture occasionally while marinating. Don't worry about letting the tomatoes sit out too long. The longer they marinate, the better.

Preheat oven to 450°F. Slice the baguette diagonally, making slices about ½ inch thick. Coat 1 side of each slice with olive oil using a pastry brush. Place bread slices on a cookie sheet, oil side down. Place bread in the oven on the top rack. Toast for 5 to 6 minutes, until the bread just begins to turn golden brown.

Remove from oven, top with bruschetta mixture, sprinkle with Parmigiano-Reggiano and serve.

GREEN OLIVE AND CREAM CHEESE TOASTS

Directions

Preheat oven to 375°F.

Cut 20 to 30 rounds from bread slices with a biscuit cutter and place on cookie sheet. Brush top side of toasts with butter and bake until golden, about 7-9 minutes.

Preheat broiler.

Mix together cream cheese, olives, scallion, paprika, white wine, and Parmigiano-Reggiano until combined well. Spread mixture on toasts. Broil until cheese begins to turn golden, 1-2 minutes.

Servings: 20 to 30 toasts

2 loaves white sandwich bread

½ stick butter, melted

8 ounces cream cheese, softened

⅓ cup green olives, chopped

4 scallions, finely chopped

1 teaspoon paprika

2 tablespoons white wine

1 cup Parmigiano-Reggiano cheese, shredded

JALAPEÑO AND ROASTED RED PEPPER CROSTINI

Servings: 20 toast slices

- ½ cup jarred roasted red bell pepper, chopped
- 1 jalapeño
- ¾ cup mayonnaise
- 2 teaspoons Worcestershire sauce
- ¼ teaspoon cayenne pepper
- ¼ teaspoon paprika
- 16 ounces sharp cheddar cheese, grated
- Kosher salt and freshly ground black pepper, to taste
- 1 French baguette, cut into ½-inch slices

Directions

Set oven to broil. Slice jalapeño vertically and lay skin side up on a foil-lined baking sheet. Broil until charred and blistered, approximately 5 minutes. Transfer to a medium bowl and cover with plastic wrap. Let steam 10 minutes.

Peel and seed jalapeño, then finely chop. Mix mayonnaise, Worcestershire sauce, cayenne, and paprika in a medium bowl. Fold in cheese and chopped peppers; season with salt and pepper.

Spread mixture on bread slices and bake for 6 minutes at 350°F. Turn the oven to broil, and broil 1 to 2 minutes, until cheese starts to brown.

(MAKE ONE GET ONE) DINNER: DAY ONE

MENU

Rosemary and Garlic–Infused Pot Roast

Baked Mashed Potatoes

Winter is the ultimate time for braising—it makes your house smell heavenly and creates a cozy atmosphere the moment you step in from the cold. The scent of this cola-braised beef will have your taste buds singing, just waiting for a bite. What's more, you can turn the leftovers into a completely different dish that's equally good. Two for one? I say yes.

ROSEMARY AND GARLIC–INFUSED POT ROAST

Servings: 4 to 6

- 4- to 5-pound boneless chuck roast
- 2 tablespoons salt
- 1 tablespoon black pepper
- 2 teaspoons kosher salt, divided
- 2 tablespoons minced garlic
- 2 teaspoons minced fresh rosemary leaves
- 2 teaspoons minced fresh sage
- 2 tablespoons vegetable oil
- 1 cup red wine
- 8 ounces rootbeer
- 12 ounces cola
- ½ cup tomato paste
- 2 cups beef stock
- 3 tablespoons flour

Directions

Preheat the oven to 325°F.

Season the roast well on all sides with salt and pepper.

Mince garlic, rosemary, and sage. Set aside.

Heat a Dutch oven over medium-high heat and add the oil. When the oil is hot, add the roast and cook until very well browned on all sides, 10 to 15 minutes. Remove roast from Dutch oven and set aside.

Add minced garlic, rosemary, and sage. Stir for 30 seconds.

Add the red wine, rootbeer, and tomato paste and stir to blend.

Add roast back to Dutch oven and add the beef stock and 1 cup of water. Bring to a boil.

Cover the Dutch oven, place in oven, and roast about 3½ hours, turning the meat every hour and adding extra water if necessary to keep the liquid level about half way up the side of the roast.

When the meat is fork-tender, remove the roast from the oven and transfer to a serving platter. Cover loosely to keep warm.

Reserve ½ cup of the liquid in a small bowl and add the flour. Stir to make a smooth paste.

Whisk this mixture into the hot cooking liquid that remains in the Dutch oven, and place over high heat on the stovetop. Cook, whisking frequently, until mixture comes to a boil and thickens into gravy, about 5 to 10 minutes. Turn down to simmer until ready to serve. Taste and adjust seasoning if necessary.

Slice the braised beef and pour gravy over the top.

Serve with baked mashed potatoes (recipe follows).

BAKED MASHED POTATOES

Servings: 6 to 8

5 pounds potatoes

1 package (8 ounces) cream cheese

1 stick (½ cup) butter

1 cup half-and-half

1 teaspoon onion salt

1 tablespoon seasoning salt

Salt and black pepper, to taste

Directions

Peel and boil potatoes for 20 to 25 minutes, or until soft when pierced with a fork. Drain potatoes and add to a large mixing bowl. Add remaining ingredients and blend together with a mixer until smooth. Put potatoes in a baking dish and refrigerate for at least an hour.

Bake uncovered at 350°F for 1 ½ hours.

MOGO

(MAKE ONE GET ONE) DINNER: DAY TWO

MENU

Braised Beef Ragout with Pappardelle

Use leftover braised beef from the Rosemary and Garlic-Infused Pot Roast (page 99) to make this ragout. Serve it over wide noodles called pappardelle. It is full of flavor, and you can prepare it in no time.

BRAISED BEEF RAGOUT
WITH PAPPARDELLE

Servings: 6 to 8

- Leftover Rosemary and Garlic-Infused Pot Roast (page 99)
- 1 can (15 ounces) diced tomatoes
- 1 can (6 ounces) tomato paste
- 1 cup beef stock
- ½ cup full-bodied red wine
- Salt and black pepper, to taste
- 1 package (16 ounces) pappardelle noodles
- 1 cup grated Parmesan cheese

Directions

Place a large skillet or Dutch oven over medium-high heat. Add leftover braised beef and diced tomatoes, shredding the meat with back of a wooden spoon as it heats.

Next, add tomato paste, beef stock, and wine. Bring to a boil and simmer until sauce cooks down and flavors meld, 30 to 45 minutes. Season to taste with salt and pepper.

While sauce is cooking, boil pappardelle according to directions.

Add noodles and Parmesan cheese to sauce.

Serve with French bread and salad.

Backyard Bash

MENU

Cajun-Rubbed Fish Tacos with Tomatillo Sauce and Pico de Gallo

Mexican Black Beans

Entertaining outdoors has to be one of the best ways to dine and socialize. I swear, food just tastes better outside. The summer months in Minnesota come and go before we know it, so we really make the most of our backyard while we can. Here is a fun way to host a backyard dinner; make fish tacos with plenty of condiments to spice things up. I am a condiment fanatic and use any chance I can to dollop a spoonful of sauce onto my meals.

CAJUN-RUBBED FISH TACOS

WITH TOMATILLO SAUCE AND PICO DE GALLO

Servings: 4 to 6

For the fish:

1 pound halibut or other mild white fish

2 to 3 tablespoons Cajun seasoning

3 tablespoons olive oil

For the tomatillo sauce:

½ cup roughly chopped cilantro

2 tomatillos, husked and chopped

1 jalapeño, seeded and chopped

2 garlic cloves, minced

Juice of 1 lime

1 cup sour cream

¼ cup mayonnaise

Salt and black pepper, to taste

For the pico de gallo:

4 to 5 tomatoes, chopped

¼ cup minced green onion

½ cup finely chopped red onion

½ to ¾ cup chopped cilantro

1 to 2 jalapeños (to taste), finely minced

Juice of 1 lime

1 to 2 garlic cloves, minced or pressed

2 teaspoons kosher salt

For the taco assembly:

Flour tortillas

Shredded cabbage

Shredded cheddar cheese

Directions

Cut fish into 2-ounce portions about ¼ to ½ inch thick. Sprinkle Cajun seasoning on both sides. Heat a large skillet over medium-high heat. Add olive oil. Add fish and cook 2 to 3 minutes per side. (The fish is thin, so don't overcook!) Place cooked fish on cookie sheet and keep warm in 250°F oven until all the fish is done.

Mix all tomatillo sauce ingredients in a food processor or blender. Place in refrigerator until ready to use.

Mix all pico de gallo ingredients together. Taste to adjust seasonings.

Warm the tortillas. For each taco, place fish, cabbage, cheese, sauce, and pico de gallo in a warm tortilla.

MEXICAN BLACK BEANS

Servings: 6

1 tablespoon canola oil

½ cup diced onion

4 cloves garlic, minced

1 jalapeño, seeded and diced

2 tablespoons tomato paste

1 bay leaf

2 cans (15 ounces) black beans, drained and rinsed

1 can (14 ounces) chicken broth

1 teaspoon chili powder

2 teaspoons cumin

1 teaspoon oregano

Salt and black pepper, to taste

Juice of ½ fresh lime

1 tablespoon chopped cilantro

Directions

Heat a medium skillet over medium heat and add the canola oil. Add onion and cook until translucent.

Stir in the garlic, jalapeño, tomato paste, and bay leaf and cook for 1 minute. Add the beans, chicken broth, chili powder, cumin, and oregano.

Simmer over low heat, stirring occasionally, until flavors meld and most of the broth has been absorbed, about 20 minutes.

Remove bay leaf. Season to taste with salt and pepper.

Squeeze a little fresh lime juice over each serving and sprinkle with cilantro.

Sharing Plates

MENU

Mussels Mariniere with Grilled Sourdough

New Orleans–Style Shrimp with Grilled Sourdough

Simple sharing plates appear often at my family's table. We like the idea of digging in together, sopping up sauce, and not bothering with utensils. There's something wonderful in the simplicity of it all. These dishes are for when you want easy, flavorful, and simple food.

The flavors and heat in this shrimp are Cajun-y good. This dish makes dunking grilled bread a heavenly adventure. Open a yummy bottle of wine on your patio and dig in.

The French mussels are fast food at its best. If you've never made mussels at home, you should really try out this recipe. It's one of our family favorites because grilled sourdough dipped in this briny, savory sauce laced with lemon, parsley, shallots, and white wine is so addicting, you'll want to double dip. Plus, mussels are inexpensive and elegant, and the dish comes together in fifteen minutes. Can't beat that.

MUSSELS MARINIERE
WITH GRILLED SOURDOUGH

Directions

Melt butter in a large Dutch oven over medium-low heat. Add shallots, garlic, red pepper flakes, and bay leaves. Season with salt and pepper and cook, stirring, until vegetables are very soft, 5 to 10 minutes.

Increase heat to high and add wine. Bring to a boil and let reduce by half, about 2 minutes. Whisk in cream (if desired), then add mussels and stir, cover, and cook, shaking pan constantly and peeking every 30 seconds to stir. As soon as all the mussels are open, they are done. This should take 2 to 3 minutes.

Add parsley and lemon juice. Stir to combine.

To grill sourdough bread, drizzle with olive oil and toast on grill 2 to 3 minutes a side. Alternatively, place bread on a cookie sheet and broil 3 to 5 minutes.

Transfer mussels to a warm serving bowl. Serve immediately with grilled bread.

Farm-raised mussels are generally quite clean when they are sold, but you'll still want to scrub them under cold water and discard any that are cracked or open.

Servings: 4

2 tablespoons butter

2 shallots, minced

4 garlic cloves, minced

½ teaspoon red pepper flakes

2 bay leaves

Kosher salt and freshly ground black pepper, to taste

1 cup white wine

2 to 3 tablespoons heavy cream (optional)

2 pounds mussels, cleaned

3 tablespoons minced fresh parsley leaves

1 tablespoon freshly squeezed lemon juice

1 loaf sourdough bread

Olive oil for drizzling

NEW ORLEANS–STYLE SHRIMP

WITH GRILLED SOURDOUGH

Servings: 4

1 loaf sourdough bread, sliced

2 tablespoons olive oil

20 large (16-20) shrimp, peeled and deveined

1 bunch of green onions, chopped

½ cup white wine

3 cloves garlic, chopped

2 tablespoons Worcestershire sauce

1 teaspoon Tabasco sauce

½ teaspoon cayenne

2 teaspoons paprika

1 stick (½ cup) of butter, cut or divided into tablespoons

Salt and black pepper, to taste

Directions

Heat grill over high heat. Grill each side of bread 2 -3 minutes until grill marks form. Remove from grill and set aside.

Place a large skillet over high heat. Add oil and cook shrimp until they are just done, 3 to 5 minutes. Remove shrimp and set aside.

Add green onions to the oil in the skillet and cook for 3 to 4 minutes. Add white wine and let simmer until it is reduced by half, 2 minutes.

When the wine is reduced, add garlic, Worcestershire, Tabasco, cayenne, and paprika. Shake the pan well and cook for 1 minute. Reduce the heat to low.

Cut butter into small chunks and slowly add into pan, shaking fast to melt butter. Add shrimp back to pan, and toss well to coat shrimp with butter and seasonings and to heat the shrimp. Season with salt and pepper. Place shrimp in a large bowl alongside bread and enjoy.

Family-Style Meal
WITH FRIENDS

MENU

Tuscan Chicken with Porcini and Sage

Peas and Prosciutto

The recipe requests I get most often are from friends looking for tasty food they can make ahead of time. They don't want the fuss of cooking and hosting at the same time.

This meal takes away that fuss. You can have the chicken cooking in the oven when your guests arrive.

The flavors of sage and porcini mushrooms elevate this simple one-pot dish. The first bite will transport you to the Tuscan countryside, and your dinner will be nothing short of divine.

TUSCAN CHICKEN
WITH PORCINI AND SAGE

Servings: 4 to 6

- 1 ounce dried porcini mushrooms
- 1 cup hot water
- 2 tablespoons butter, divided
- 2 tablespoons olive oil, divided
- ½ cup all-purpose flour
- 1 teaspoon paprika
- 1 teaspoon salt, plus extra for seasoning
- ½ teaspoon black pepper, plus extra for seasoning
- 1 whole cut-up chicken
- 3 cloves garlic, minced
- 2 tablespoons minced fresh sage
- 1 cup dry red wine
- 1 can (14 ounces) crushed tomatoes
- 1 cup chicken stock
- 3 tablespoons tomato paste
- 1 cup frozen peas
- Salt and black pepper, to taste

Directions

Soak dried mushrooms in 1 cup of hot water for 30 minutes. Drain broth and set aside. Chop mushrooms.

In a Dutch oven, heat 1 tablespoon of butter and 1 tablespoon of olive oil over medium-high heat. In a large skillet, heat remaining butter and olive oil. (You will need 2 pans to fry all the chicken.)

Mix flour, paprika, salt, and pepper together on a plate. Salt and pepper the chicken and dredge the pieces in the flour mixture. Sauté the chicken, skin side down, until golden, 7 to 8 minutes. Turn chicken and sear an additional 3 minutes. Remove and set aside.

Next, add the garlic and sage to the pan and stir for 30 seconds. Add the wine, tomatoes, reserved mushroom broth, and chicken stock and season generously with salt and pepper. Bring the mixture to a boil and add mushrooms and tomato paste. Reduce sauce for 5 minutes. Turn off heat and add the chicken to the pot. Cover the Dutch oven and cook in the oven at 350°F for 45 minutes. Remove from oven, place chicken on the platter, and adjust seasonings. Serve with your favorite pasta.

PEAS AND PROSCIUTTO

Servings: 4 to 6

2 tablespoons olive oil

⅓ cup chopped shallots

4 ounces thinly sliced prosciutto, diced

1 bag (16 ounces) frozen peas

Salt and black pepper, to taste

Directions

In a large skillet over medium heat, heat the olive oil, then add the shallots. Sauté 1 to 2 minutes or until the shallots start to get translucent.

Add the prosciutto and sauté 3 minutes, until prosciutto starts to crisp.

Add the peas to the skillet. Heat through, stirring frequently, about 5 minutes.

Season with salt and pepper. Serve immediately.

My Big Fat Greek Feast

MENU

Chicken Souvlaki with Tzatziki

Greek Salad

Saffron Rice

I have a confession: I love street food. On a trip to Greece, I encountered what would become my favorite street food of all time. I came across these fun little carts selling souvlaki, which is the Greek version of fast food. The street vendors would carve this wonderfully seasoned meat off a spit, pour tzatziki (yogurt sauce) over the top, and add the freshest chunks of tomato, cucumber, and onion. It was simply wonderful.

Here I've created a menu to replicate those wonderful flavors of Greece. These recipes are great for when you're having guests over because much of them can be made ahead. If you don't want to make homemade tzatziki, simply pick some up from your favorite grocer.

CHICKEN SOUVLAKI
WITH TZATZIKI

Servings: 6

For the chicken:

2 pounds chicken, cut into one-inch cubes for grilling

½ cup fresh (or bottled) lemon juice

¼ cup red wine vinegar

¼ cup olive oil

1 teaspoon salt

1 teaspoon freshly ground black pepper

2 tablespoons fresh oregano, chopped

4 teaspoons minced garlic

For the tzatziki:

2 containers (8 ounces) plain Greek yogurt

2 cucumbers, peeled, seeded, and diced

2 tablespoons olive oil

Juice of ½ lemon

Salt and black pepper, to taste

1 tablespoon chopped fresh dill

3 cloves garlic, minced

For sandwich assembly:

Pita bread

Shredded lettuce

Tomatoes

Directions

Place the chicken in a large resealable plastic bag. In a bowl, mix together the lemon juice, vinegar, oil, salt, pepper, oregano, and garlic, and pour over the meat. Chill at least 2 hours and up to overnight.

Preheat grill. Drain the marinade off the chicken. Skewer the chicken and place on grill over medium-high heat until cooked through, 10 to 15 minutes, rotating chicken occasionally. Remove from the grill.

Mix the tzatziki ingredients together and stir well. Cover and refrigerate until ready to use.

Place pita bread on the grill until just warmed through, approximately 1-2 minutes a side. To assemble each sandwich, top pita with chicken, lettuce, tomatoes, and tzatziki. Serve immediately.

GREEK SALAD

Servings: 6 to 8

For the vinaigrette:

2 cloves garlic, minced

1 teaspoon dried oregano

½ teaspoon Dijon mustard

¼ cup good red wine vinegar

1 teaspoon kosher salt

1 teaspoon freshly ground black pepper

½ cup good olive oil

For the salad:

2 seedless cucumbers, peeled and sliced ¼ inch thick

1 red bell pepper, large diced

1 yellow bell pepper, large diced

6 to 8 whole pepperoncinis, halved

1 pint cherry or grape tomatoes, halved

½ red onion, halved then sliced

Salt and black pepper, to taste

½ pound feta cheese, diced in ½-inch pieces (not crumbled)

½ cup kalamata olives, pitted

Directions

For the vinaigrette, whisk together the garlic, oregano, mustard, vinegar, salt, and pepper in your serving bowl. Still whisking, slowly add the olive oil to make an emulsion. Place the cucumber, peppers, tomatoes, and onion in a large bowl. Salt and pepper to taste.

Add the feta and olives and toss lightly.

Set aside for 30 minutes to allow the flavors to blend. Serve at room temperature.

When making salads, mix the dressing right in the serving bowl. It mixes well and is easy to toss with the salad.

SAFFRON RICE

Servings: 6

1 teaspoon saffron threads

2 tablespoons hot water

2 cups chicken or vegetable broth

2 tablespoons olive oil

½ cup diced onions

1 cup jasmine rice

1 teaspoon salt

1 cup green peas

Directions

Soak saffron in hot water for 10 minutes. In a medium-sized pot, combine saffron and chicken stock, bring to a boil, and simmer for 2 minutes.

In a medium skillet over medium-high heat, add olive oil. Next add onions and cook until translucent, 5 to 8 minutes. Add rice and salt and sauté for 1 to 2 minutes.

Pour onion and rice mixture into chicken stock and bring to a boil. Once the mixture starts boiling, immediately cover and turn to low heat.

Let the rice cook on low heat, undisturbed, for 20 minutes. Turn off heat. Add peas and let sit for another 5 to 8 minutes, covered, to finish cooking by steaming. Use a fork to fluff up the rice and serve.

Hot Date Night at Home

(ONE GLASS OF WINE PREP)

MENU

Fettuccine with Peas and Proscuitto

Cooking together with your significant other can be intimate, romantic, and fun. Enjoying a glass of wine, your favorite music, wonderful smells wafting from your stovetop, and of course each other allows you to slow things down a bit and relax.

As I've mentioned before, my husband and I started cooking together early on in our marriage, when little babies entered the scene and babysitters were scarce. After the kids went to bed, we'd spend a romantic evening making dinner and trying to recreate all the restaurant dishes we were used to having out.

Here are two delicious meals you can try, depending on the time you have. They are just as good as going out. I hope you try both!

FETTUCCINE
WITH PEAS AND PROSCIUTTO

Servings: 4 to 6

1 tablespoon olive oil

1 tablespoon unsalted butter

1 shallot, minced

1 tablespoon garlic, minced

2 ounces prosciutto, diced

¼ cup dry white wine

1 ½ cups heavy cream

¾ teaspoon salt

½ teaspoon fresh cracked black pepper

¾ cup frozen sweet peas

1 pound fresh or packaged fettuccine

¾ cup grated Parmigiano-Reggiano

Drizzle of truffle oil (optional)

Directions

Set a large pot of water over high heat and bring to a boil.

Meanwhile, set a large sauté pan over medium-high heat and add the olive oil and the butter. Add the shallot to the pan and sauté until translucent, about 3 minutes. Add the garlic to the pan and sauté for 30 seconds. Place the prosciutto in the pan and sauté for 3 to 5 minutes. Deglaze the pan with wine and cook until it is nearly evaporated, about 30 seconds. Add the cream, salt, and pepper to the pan, and cook 4 to 5 minutes, letting the cream reduce by half. Add the peas.

When the pot of water is boiling, stir in the pasta. Turn the sauce to low while the pasta cooks. Strain the pasta and place in sauce. Sprinkle with the cheese. Drizzle with truffle oil. Toss the pasta well. Serve immediately.

Hot Date Night at Home

(TWO GLASSES OF WINE PREP)

MENU

Red Wine Risotto with Seared Scallops

This recipe for scallops on a bed of risotto is a simple yet elegant way to make dinner special. I want to debunk the myth that risotto is an impossibly hard dish to make. I promise it's not! And in fact, it can be one of the most relaxing dishes to cook. Make this meal when you have time to slow down and stir some love into your pot of risotto.

Make sure you taste the risotto before you finish cooking so your rice isn't hard. It may take more than 30 minutes, and you may need more chicken stock, so don't be afraid to add some.

RED WINE RISOTTO
WITH SEARED SCALLOPS

Servings: 2 to 4

½ cup favorite red wine

1 quart chicken stock

2 tablespoons butter

2 large shallots, chopped

1 carrot, diced

1 celery stalk, diced

4 garlic cloves, minced

1 ½ cups uncooked Arborio rice

1 teaspoon salt

1 teaspoon pepper

1 tablespoon chopped fresh parsley

6 to 8 scallops

1 cup flour

1 tablespoon olive oil

¾ cup Parmesan cheese

Directions

Heat wine and stock in a large saucepan over medium heat.

In a large skillet, melt butter over medium-high heat. Add shallots, carrot, celery, and garlic, and a teaspoon of salt and pepper, and sauté until tender, about 5 minutes.

Add rice and sauté, stirring constantly, for 1 minute.

Reduce heat to medium; add ½ cup hot wine mixture (or a ladleful); cook, stirring frequently, until liquid is absorbed. Repeat procedure with remaining wine mixture, ½ cup at a time. (Cooking time is 30 to 45 minutes.)

Season to taste again with salt and pepper. Add parsley; keep warm.

Rinse scallops and pat dry. Line a plate with paper towels and place the scallops on the towels. Pour flour on a plate. Dust the scallops and then season with salt and pepper.

Heat large nonstick skillet over high heat. Once hot, add olive oil, swirling to coat the base of the pan. Place the scallops into the pan and let them cook undisturbed for a good 2 to 3 minutes, without touching them, to get a good sear. Turn and cook for another 2 minutes.

Scoop risotto into the center of each plate, sprinkle with Parmesan cheese, and add scallops on top.

Coworkers for Dinner

MENU

Fioretti Caesar Salad

Penne with Sausage, Peas, and Mascarpone

When I was growing up, my dad worked with a guy by the name of Ed Fioretti. Ed became one of my dad's best friends. I'll never forget the first time I met him. Dad had invited him to our house for dinner. Ed lived in Chicago. He was Italian, good-looking, and drove a flashy red convertible that my sister and I got to drive—much to my dad's chagrin. Ed adored my mom and loved to give her a hard time in the kitchen. He said he was going to show her how to make a "real" Caesar salad. A man cooking in our kitchen? I was impressed. Ed has since passed away, but his salad recipe lives on. It's one of the things that inspired me to cook, and it remains one of my faves, so I had to share it with all of you.

For the salad, use a wooden bowl if you have one. It absorbs the anchovy-garlic flavor best.

The penne recipe gets its richness from Italian sausage, cream, and mascarpone cheese. It is one of my favorites when I'm looking for a hearty pasta dish. Incorporating roasted red peppers and peas gives it the perfect balance of flavors.

FIORETTI CAESAR SALAD

Servings: 6

3 cloves garlic, minced

½ can (1 ounce) anchovies (optional)

¼ cup olive oil

1 teaspoon dry mustard

2 teaspoons Worcestershire sauce

1 egg (pasteurized, if possible)

3 shakes of Tabasco sauce

Salt and black pepper, to taste

2 bunches romaine

1 cup croutons

½ cup Parmigiano-Reggiano cheese

Directions

Place garlic and anchovies in a bowl. With a wooden spoon, mash the garlic and anchovies against the sides of the bowl to make a paste.

Mix together olive oil, mustard, Worcestershire sauce, egg, and Tabasco sauce in a small bowl. Add mixture to salad bowl and mix together to make the dressing. Season with salt and pepper.

Wash and chop romaine. Place lettuce in bowl along with croutons. Toss well. Sprinkle with cheese and serve.

PENNE
WITH SAUSAGE, PEAS, AND MASCARPONE

Servings: 6 to 8

1 pound mild Italian sausage, ground

1 cup chopped onion

1 cup heavy whipping cream

1 cup canned low-salt chicken broth

1 can (28 ounces) fire-roasted tomatoes, crushed

½ cup roasted red peppers, chopped

½ to 1 teaspoon red pepper flakes

1 pound penne pasta

⅔ cup mascarpone cheese

2 cups frozen peas

2 tablespoons chopped parsley

¾ cup freshly grated Parmesan cheese

Salt and black pepper, to taste

Directions

Sauté sausage in Dutch oven over high heat until brown, breaking into small pieces with back of spoon, about 12 minutes. Using slotted spoon, transfer sausage to bowl.

Pour off all but 1 tablespoon of sausage drippings. Add onion and sauté until light brown, about 6 minutes. Add cream; boil 5 minutes. Add broth and simmer until reduced to sauce consistency, stirring occasionally, about 8 minutes. Return sausage to pot along with tomatoes, red pepper flakes, and roasted red pepper.

Cook penne in large pot of boiling salted water until pasta is just tender but still firm to bite.

Meanwhile, bring sauce to simmer over medium heat. Add peas and mascarpone and simmer until peas are tender, about 5 minutes.

Drain pasta. Add to sauce; toss to coat. Sprinkle with parsley and Parmesan. Season with salt and pepper. Transfer to large bowl and serve.

RESTAURANT-INSPIRED MEALS

Restaurants are a big inspiration in my cooking. Dining out is one of my favorite hobbies. I love trying new restaurants—fancy restaurants as well as dives. I love reading about new chefs and finding out who's opening new places in the Twin Cities. I love restaurants with open kitchens. You'll find me sitting at the kitchen counter so I can watch all the action.

It's always fun to try new dishes and new ingredients and take them back into the kitchen. I've called many restaurants to ask for recipes for dishes I've had. Chefs have been so generous to me and have happily e-mailed recipes upon request. It's so fun to learn new techniques.

The recipes in this chapter are from meals I've had out and absolutely loved—112 Eatery, Spoon and Stable, Prima, and the Kenwood Inn and Spa, to name a few. These are revised for the home cook and are great way to enjoy restaurant cooking in the comfort of your own kitchen.

Mexican Night
(WHEN YOU WISH YOU WERE IN CABO)

MENU

Chicken Enchiladas with Tomatillo Sour Cream Sauce

Something about Mexican food always makes me feel festive, and our family is not shy about trying new Mexican recipes. This is our go-to recipe for enchiladas, and the tomatillo sour cream sauce is addicting. These enchiladas will not stay around long. Make two batches and freeze some for later.

Chopping the chicken in a food processor makes the enchiladas more restaurant-quality and also makes it easier to roll the tortillas.

You can freeze any leftover chicken for another use.

If the enchiladas won't all fit in your baking dish, put the extras in a smaller dish and freeze for later.

CHICKEN ENCHILADAS
WITH TOMATILLO SOUR CREAM SAUCE

Servings: 6 to 8 (16 to 18 enchiladas)

For the filling:

4 boneless, skinless chicken breasts

1 teaspoon kosher salt

1 teaspoon black pepper

1 tablespoon olive oil

For the sauce:

2 tablespoons unsalted butter

2 jalapeños, diced

2 cloves garlic, minced

2 tablespoons all-purpose flour

2 cups chicken broth

2 cups sour cream

1 teaspoon ground cumin

⅛ teaspoon cayenne

1 cup loosely chopped cilantro

Salt and black pepper, to taste

1 can (10 ounces) tomatillos

For the enchiladas:

18 flour tortillas

2 cups Chihuahua or Monterey Jack cheese

½ medium-size red onion, diced

½ cup chopped cilantro, for serving

Directions

Preheat the oven to 350°F.

Place chicken breasts on a foil-lined cookie sheet. Sprinkle breasts with salt and pepper and drizzle with olive oil. Bake chicken for 35 to 45 minutes, depending on how large the breasts are. Roughly chop chicken and then pulse in a food processor to finely chop. If you don't have a food processor, finely chop chicken with a knife.

To make the sauce, melt the butter in a saucepan on medium-low. Add jalapeños and cook until soft, 4 to 5 minutes. Add the garlic and cook for another minute. Whisk in the flour and cook for 1 more minute. Pour the chicken broth into the pot, bring to a boil, and then reduce to a simmer. Whisk frequently and cook until the chicken broth has thickened, 8 to 10 minutes. Stir in the sour cream, cumin, cayenne, and cilantro. Remove from heat.

Place the sour cream mixture in a blender along with the tomatillos. Blend until smooth. Alternatively, if you have an immersion blender, you can add tomatillos to saucepan and mix.

To assemble the enchiladas, first warm the flour tortillas in the microwave for 30 seconds so they are pliable. Next, pour 1 cup of the sauce in the bottom of a large baking dish. Place in the middle of each tortilla ⅓ cup of shredded chicken and 1 to 2 tablespoons of cheese. Roll the tortillas around the filling, and place the rolled tortillas seam side down in the dish. Cover the enchiladas with the remaining sauce and cheese and bake for 25 minutes or until the topping is brown and bubbling. Sprinkle with onion and cilantro before serving.

MENU

Lamb Chops with Herbes de Provence and Yogurt Pesto

Crispy Roasted Rosemary Potatoes with Sour Cream Chive Sauce

One of my favorite restaurants in Minneapolis is 112 Eatery. After all these years, my husband and I seem to end up there when we are looking for incredible food in a casual environment. Our first time at 112 Eatery we ordered the lamb *scottadito* with goat's milk yogurt, and I was in heaven. I went home the next day to try to recreate the dish, and I wound up using herbes de Provence and making a new sauce with Greek yogurt and pesto. This meal turned into one of our favorites. So before you skip over this recipe because you don't like lamb, just try it once. These chops are pounded out thin and marinated. You can make them in advance for low-stress prep, and by the end of the night, you and your guests will be licking the sauce off your plates. Add a loaf of crusty ciabatta and dig in.

LAMB CHOPS

WITH HERBES DE PROVENCE AND YOGURT PESTO

Servings: 2 to 4

For the sauce:

1 cup plain Greek yogurt

¼ to ½ cup pesto

Salt and black pepper, to taste

1 tablespoon lemon juice

For the lamb:

1 single rack of lamb

Salt and black pepper, to taste

½ cup of olive oil

4 to 5 tablespoons herbes de Provence

Directions:

Mix all sauce ingredients together. You can make this 1 day ahead.

Next, slice rack of lamb into individual chops, and pound out each chop between plastic wrap, ¼ inch thick. (You can have a butcher do this, too.) Salt and pepper both sides.

In a bowl, make a paste by mixing herbes de Provence and olive oil. Rub paste on both sides of lamb chops. Put into a resealable plastic bag and marinate at least 1 hour.

Grill chops 3 to 4 minutes per side. Place grilled chops on a platter and pour the yogurt pesto sauce over them. Serve immediately.

CRISPY ROASTED ROSEMARY POTATOES

WITH SOUR CREAM CHIVE SAUCE

Servings: 4 to 6

For the potatoes:

8 medium red potatoes

½ red onion, diced

2 tablespoons chopped fresh rosemary

4 garlic cloves, minced

Salt and black pepper, to taste

¼ cup olive oil

¼ cup Parmigiano-Reggiano cheese

For the sauce:

1 cup sour cream

2 tablespoons minced chives

Dash of salt and black pepper

Introduction

Sometimes a great side dish can be the star of the show. That's why these potatoes—crispy, earthy, with a hint of rosemary and garlic—are a staple at our house, and the chive sour cream sauce adds to every savory bite. These can go with any meat or seafood, and the leftovers are perfect with a poached or fried egg for breakfast the next morning.

When roasting potatoes, place the cookie sheet in the oven during preheating so the sheet gets piping hot. It helps prevent your potatoes from sticking.

Directions

Place cookie sheet in oven and heat to 400°F. Cut the potatoes in ¼-inch chunks and put in a large bowl. Mix the diced red onion, rosemary, garlic, salt, pepper, and olive oil separately. Pour over potatoes and mix together.

Bake uncovered 30 minutes. After 30 minutes, stir potatoes to cook evenly and prevent from sticking. Bake an additional 20-30 minutes and stir the potatoes once more. Sprinkle with cheese for the last 10 to 15 minutes of baking. Transfer to serving bowl.

Mix together ingredients for sour cream chive sauce and serve alongside potatoes.

A Night in Paris

MENU

One-Skillet Rosemary Chicken with Lemon Garlic Cream Sauce

French Green Beans with Pancetta

French farm cooks use lots of shallots in their cooking. I always have a bunch on hand. I love their sweet, intense flavor, and they work particularly well in dishes made with wine. Gotta love the French! This dish comes together beautifully in one skillet. I serve this with a green bean sauté and crusty French bread.

ONE-SKILLET ROSEMARY CHICKEN

WITH LEMON GARLIC CREAM SAUCE

Directions

Preheat the oven to 375°F.

Cover chicken breasts with plastic wrap; using a mallet, pound chicken into ½-inch thickness, or have your butcher do this for you. Season both sides of breasts with salt and pepper.

In large measuring cup or a small bowl, combine the chicken broth, white wine, lemon juice, garlic, rosemary, and red pepper flakes.

Heat the olive oil in a large skillet over medium-high heat. Add the chicken and allow to brown on both sides for 2 to 3 minutes per side. Don't worry if the chicken isn't cooked completely; it will finish in the oven. Remove the chicken to a plate.

Reduce the flame to medium, add the shallots to the skillet, and sauté 1 to 2 minutes. Add the chicken broth mixture. Using a whisk, scrape the bottom of the pan to loosen all the brown bits. Let sauce reduce for 7 to 8 minutes or until about ⅓ cup of the sauce remains.

When the sauce has thickened, turn skillet down to low heat and add the butter; whisk until it melts completely. Next, add the cream and whisk to combine. Remove from heat, add the chicken back into the pan, and drizzle the sauce over the chicken. Place the skillet in the oven for 5 to 8 minutes or until the chicken is completely cooked through. Top with chopped parsley and serve warm with lemon slices.

Servings: 4

4 boneless, skinless chicken breasts

Salt and black pepper, to taste

1 cup chicken broth

¼ cup white wine

2 tablespoons lemon juice

2 garlic cloves, minced

1 tablespoon minced rosemary

½ teaspoon red pepper flakes (or more to taste)

2 tablespoons olive oil

⅓ cup finely diced shallots

2 tablespoons salted butter

⅓ cup heavy cream

2 tablespoons chopped parsley

1 lemon, sliced

FRENCH GREEN BEANS
WITH PANCETTA

Servings: 4 to 6

- 8 ounces pancetta, diced small
- 2 shallots, minced
- 2 pounds green beans, trimmed and blanched until almost tender
- Salt and freshly ground black pepper, to taste

Directions

In a large skillet over medium heat, cook the pancetta until browned and crispy, about 8 minutes. Using a slotted spoon, transfer the pancetta to a paper towel–lined plate. Set aside.

Return the pan to medium heat. Add the shallots and cook, stirring occasionally, until tender, 3 to 5 minutes. Add the green beans and cook, stirring often, until tender, 3 to 5 minutes. Stir in the pancetta and season with salt and pepper.

Fancy Burger Night

MENU

Asian Turkey Burgers with Sriracha Aioli and Crunchy Lime Slaw

Hot Szechuan-Style Green Beans

You can elevate burger night with this Asian twist on a turkey burger. These burgers are even fancy enough for your next casual dinner party. Hoisin sauce gives these burgers a juicy texture, while ginger, garlic, and sambal oelek provide a burst of flavor. The cabbage adds a crunchy bite, and the sriracha aioli makes these burgers insanely good.

The Szechuan-style green beans are so addicting, you'll probably end up eating them as an appetizer while the burgers are grilling. So simple to make, these are a healthy and delicious side dish to the Asian-style turkey burger.

HOT SZECHUAN-STYLE GREEN BEANS

Servings: 6

1 ½ pounds green beans

3 tablespoons soy sauce

1 ½ tablespoons rice vinegar

3 teaspoons sugar

¾ teaspoon hot chili flakes

½ teaspoon white pepper

¼ cup water

1 ½ tablespoons canola oil

3 tablespoons minced garlic

3 tablespoons minced fresh ginger

Directions

Rinse and drain green beans. Trim off ends. Cut into 2-inch lengths.

In a small bowl, mix soy sauce, rice vinegar, sugar, chili flakes, and white pepper.

Heat frying pan on high. Add beans and water. Cover and cook, stirring once, until beans are bright green and slightly crunchy, approximately 3 to 5 minutes. Uncover and cook until all liquid evaporates.

Add oil, garlic, and ginger to the pan and cook briefly, 1 minute. Add soy sauce mixture and bring to a boil. Stir until the sauce thickens enough to coat the beans, 2 to 3 minutes.

ASIAN TURKEY BURGERS

WITH SRIRACHA AIOLI AND CRUNCHY LIME SLAW

Servings: 6

16 ounces ground turkey

1 egg, beaten

¾ cup plain bread crumbs

⅓ cup minced green onion

2 cloves garlic, minced

1 teaspoon ground ginger

3 teaspoons sesame seeds

2 tablespoons hoisin sauce

1 tablespoon sambal oelek, or any chili paste

1 teaspoon kosher salt

⅓ cup chopped peanuts

1 tablespoon canola oil

2 cups shredded cabbage (coleslaw mix)

1 tablespoon lime juice

½ cup mayonnaise

1 tablespoon lemon juice

1 teaspoon Dijon mustard

2 tablespoons sriracha sauce

6 hamburger buns, toasted

Directions

Mix the turkey, egg, bread crumbs, onion, garlic, ginger, sesame seeds, hoisin sauce, sambal oelek, salt, and peanuts into a large bowl. Form 6 patties and place them on a lined cookie sheet. Refrigerate until ready to cook.

Preheat a large skillet or grill to medium-high heat. Lightly oil skillet or grill. Cook the turkey burgers until no longer pink in the center and the juices run clear, about 5 minutes per side. An instant-read thermometer inserted into the center of a burger should read at least 165°F.

While burgers are cooking, mix cabbage with lime juice. Set aside.

Next, combine the mayonnaise, lemon juice, mustard, and sriracha sauce to make the sriracha aioli. Mix well and set aside.

Assemble the burgers and buns and top with cabbage and aioli.

MENU

Penne con Pollo

Italian Chopped Salad

I created this menu after a meal we had at one of our favorite Italian restaurants in Minneapolis. A head of roasted garlic, along with sun-dried tomatoes and Parmesan, makes this rotini a lovely dish for both adults and kids.

The Italian chopped salad is full of crunchy textures and dressed in creamy, tangy Italian-style vinaigrette.

PENNE CON POLLO

Servings: 6 to 8

- 1 head garlic
- 4 tablespoons olive oil, divided, plus extra for drizzling
- 1 package (16 ounces) chicken breasts
- ¼ cup Italian seasoning
- 1 cup chopped onion
- 4 ounces sun-dried tomatoes
- 3 tablespoons chopped parsley
- 3 cups chicken stock
- 1 cup cream or half-and-half
- Salt and black pepper, to taste
- 1 box (16 ounces) rotini or penne pasta
- ½ cup Parmigiano-Reggiano cheese

Directions

Slice the top off the garlic, drizzle with olive oil, wrap in aluminum foil, and cook for 1 hour at 375°F.

In the meantime, slice the chicken very thin. (It's much easier to cut the chicken when it's semi-frozen.) Put chicken in a bowl, season with salt and pepper, and add 2 tablespoons olive oil and Italian seasoning. Marinate for at least 1 hour.

Heat 2 more tablespoons of olive oil in a pan over medium-high heat, and sear chicken until cooked through, 8 to 10 minutes. Remove chicken from pan and set aside.

Add onion to oil and cook over medium heat until translucent. Then add the sun-dried tomatoes, parsley, roasted garlic, and chicken. Cook until mixed together, 3 to 4 minutes. Add the chicken stock and boil over medium-high heat until stock cooks down, 5 to 10 minutes. Add cream or half-and-half and cook down 5 to 10 minutes. Season with salt and pepper.

Cook the pasta according to package directions. Toss pasta with sauce and top with cheese to finish.

ITALIAN CHOPPED SALAD

Servings: 6 to 8

1 garlic clove, minced

2 tablespoons mayonnaise

2 tablespoons red wine vinegar

1 teaspoon Italian seasoning

1 teaspoon dried mustard

¼ cup extra-virgin olive oil

Salt and black pepper, to taste

1 head romaine, chopped

1 bag (16 ounces) mixed greens

½ small red onion, thinly sliced

½ cup cherry tomatoes

½ cup sliced pepperoni

½ cup drained and chopped artichoke hearts

5 pepperoncinis

1 cup shaved Parmigiano-Reggiano cheese

Directions

In a mason jar or salad dressing container, put garlic, mayonnaise, vinegar, Italian seasoning, and dried mustard. Slowly whisk in the olive oil. Season with salt and pepper. Place all of the remaining ingredients in a large salad bowl. Toss salad with dressing and serve.

Thai at Home

MENU

Shrimp Pad Thai

I love these wonderful, chewy, sticky-sweet yet spicy noodles. Whenever we go out for Thai food, I order this dish—unfortunately, that isn't often enough, so I learned how I could bring it to my table at home. Traditional pad thai is made with tofu and shrimp, but you can always switch it up with chicken or just veggies. You may not have fish sauce and tamarind paste on hand, but these ingredients can be found in the Asian food section of most grocery stores. This dish isn't difficult to make—it just takes a little prep time, and it's so worth it!

SHRIMP PAD THAI

Servings: 6 to 8

1 pound Thai rice noodles

1 pound medium-size shrimp, peeled and deveined

1 teaspoon cornstarch

3 tablespoons soy sauce

3 to 4 tablespoons peanut oil, divided

2 shallots, finely chopped

2 cloves garlic, minced

1 to 2 fresh red chilies, minced (optional)

1 tablespoon chili powder

¼ cup tamarind paste, reconstituted in ¼ cup water

¼ cup rice vinegar

2 tablespoons fish sauce, plus more to taste

2 tablespoons brown sugar

¼ cup creamy peanut butter

¼ cup thinly sliced green onion

¼ cup chopped cilantro leaves

¼ cup coarsely chopped peanuts

2 limes, quartered

Directions

Bring a large pot of water to a boil and remove from heat. Cook rice noodles according to instructions. Drain and set aside.

Place shrimp in a bowl. Stir together the cornstarch and soy sauce in a separate bowl. Pour this marinade over shrimp. Set aside.

Meanwhile, heat peanut oil over medium heat in a saucepan. Add the shallots, garlic, and red chilies (if using) and cook until soft. Add the chili powder and cook for 10 seconds. Add the tamarind mixture, vinegar, fish sauce, brown sugar, and peanut butter and bring to a boil. Remove sauce from heat.

Next, warm up a wok or large frying pan over medium-high heat. Add 1 to 2 tablespoons of oil. Add shrimp and stir-fry until the shrimp is cooked, 3 to 4 minutes.

Place the cooked noodles and shrimp in a large bowl. Pour the sauce over the noodles and toss gently until combined. Fold in the green onion and cilantro and top with the chopped peanuts.

Serve with limes on the side.

Napa-Inspired Luncheon

MENU

Spicy Chicken Caesar on Flatbread
with Bacon and Blue Cheese

My husband and I spent our ten-year anniversary in the beautiful Sonoma Valley at the Kenwood Inn and Spa. The Mediterranean villas amid lush surroundings and luxurious accommodations, not to mention the food, made this a favorite destination. After we arrived, we enjoyed lunch outside in their quaint Italianesque courtyard, and it was the perfect start to our vacation. We had a chicken Caesar salad on their homemade flatbread. The Kenwood Inn uses a wood-burning pizza oven for their flatbread, so it has the perfect chewiness and crunch. I loved their idea of serving salad on flatbread, so I've kicked this up with blue cheese, bacon, and Tabasco. A pizza stone is great to use if you have one. This is a perfect, leisurely lunch to share with friends or a great appetizer to share before dinner.

Pair this dish with Ferrari-Carano Fumé Blanc.

SPICY CHICKEN CAESAR ON FLATBREAD

WITH BACON AND BLUE CHEESE

Servings: 4

- 8 ounces cooked boneless, skinless chicken breasts
- 1 premade pizza dough (found at Trader Joe's)
- 2 anchovy fillets, drained
- ¼ teaspoon kosher salt
- ¼ teaspoon freshly ground black pepper, plus extra for seasoning
- 1 teaspoon chopped garlic
- 1 large egg (pasteurized, if possible)
- 2 tablespoons freshly grated Parmesan cheese
- 1 tablespoon fresh lemon juice
- 1 teaspoon Dijon mustard
- ¼ cup extra-virgin olive oil
- 1 teaspoon Worcestershire sauce
- 1 teaspoon hot pepper sauce
- 4 cups chopped romaine
- 2 cups mesclun
- ½ cup crumbled blue cheese
- 6 ounces bacon, chopped and cooked until crisp, drained

Directions

Grill or poach chicken until tender. Let it cool, then dice.

Preheat the oven to 475°F. If available, place a baking stone on the lower rack of the oven and preheat stone to 475°F. Remove the dough, place on a lightly floured work surface, and let rest for 10 minutes.

Shape dough into a 14-inch round. Transfer to the baking stone and cook in oven until the crust is golden brown, 8 to 10 minutes. Remove from oven and let cool slightly.

Meanwhile, to make the dressing, in a small bowl, combine the anchovies, salt, pepper, and garlic and mash to a paste with the back of a fork. Add the egg and whisk well to blend. Add the cheese, lemon juice, and mustard, and whisk well. Add the olive oil in a steady stream, whisking constantly to form a thick emulsion. Add the Worcestershire and pepper sauce and whisk well to combine. Cover tightly and refrigerate until ready to use. (The dressing will keep refrigerated for up to 12 hours.)

In a large bowl, combine romaine and mesclun lettuces and chicken, and toss with dressing to lightly coat. Arrange the mixture over the top of the warm pizza crust and sprinkle the top with the blue cheese and bacon. Lightly drizzle with dressing to taste.

Top with freshly ground black pepper and serve immediately.

MENU

Chicken Tikka Masala

Chicken tikka masala is created using chunks of chicken in a creamy and spicy tomato sauce. When you make this dish, your kitchen will fill with the intoxicating aromas of rich Indian spices, including garam masala, turmeric, and cumin. It's a feast for the senses and one of my favorite Indian dishes.

CHICKEN TIKKA MASALA

Servings: 6 to 8

For the marinade:

1 cup plain yogurt

2 tablespoons lime juice

1 tablespoon garam masala

2 teaspoons turmeric

1 teaspoon cumin

3 garlic cloves, minced

1 tablespoon minced fresh ginger root

1 teaspoon salt

4 boneless, skinless chicken breasts, cut into 1 ½-inch cubes

For the masala sauce:

1 medium onion, roughly chopped

2 cloves garlic, chopped

1-inch piece peeled ginger root, roughly chopped

1 whole red chile, minced

2 tablespoons butter

3 teaspoons garam masala

2 large tomatoes, finely chopped

1 can (8 ounces) tomato sauce

1 cup heavy cream

Salt and pepper, to taste

¼ cup chopped cilantro

For Serving:

Basmati rice

Naan bread

Lime wedges

Directions

Mix all marinade ingredients and pour over chicken in a large bowl. Cover with plastic wrap and refrigerate for at least 2 hours, preferably overnight.

Cook chicken in a large pan over high heat until nearly cooked through, then transfer to a plate and set aside. You'll want the chicken to finish cooking in the sauce.

To make the sauce, combine onion, garlic, ginger, and red chile in a food processor until smooth. Heat the butter in a medium saucepan, then pour in onion mixture. Add salt and cook on medium heat for 10 minutes, stirring frequently.

Add garam masala, tomatoes, and tomato sauce. Lower heat slightly and cook until tomatoes cook down into the sauce, about 15 minutes.

Add chicken and cook for another 15 minutes. Add cream and cook on low to let the sauce thicken, 5 to 10 minutes. Season again with salt and pepper to taste.

Sprinkle with cilantro and serve with basmati rice, naan, and lime wedges.

Four

WEEKNIGHT COOKING

Weeknight cooking can make even the best cooks cringe. Honestly, it'd be much easier to open a bag of tortilla chips and salsa and call it good. And believe me, I'm as much a culprit of this as anyone. I'm not one of those organized people who precuts everything on Sunday and maps out their meals with ease. Where's the fun in that? What if I change my mind and don't feel like lasagna on Thursday? But I always feel like something is missing when I don't cook *anything* for dinner.

As most of us can attest, the weeknight dinner has become more and more challenging over the years. Let's face it, we've got a lot working against us—kids' activities, spouses' work schedules, picky eaters, and not to mention actually finding time to cook. All these factors can push dinner to the bottom of our priority lists.

But I love what happens when my family slows down for a meal and comes together, even for a short time, because it connects us like nothing else. I think my family feels it, too. So my goal is to help you get dinner on the table during those busy weeknights when you need a plan in a pinch that also tastes good. Doesn't hurt if you can have fun in the process, too!

The following menus will do just that. Here is what's important: one-pot cooking, ingredients on hand, options to make ahead, a little grace on harried nights, and a great attitude.

Soup and Sandwich Night

MENU

Tomato Basil Soup

Make-Ahead Mini Croque Monsieur Sandwiches

A soup and sandwich dinner can save most of us on busy nights. I cherish my memories of dipping grilled cheese into Campbell's tomato soup when I was growing up. In this recipe, I've kicked up the traditional tomato basil soup with cayenne and gin. That's right—gin really boosts the tomato flavor, and the cayenne is my favorite chef's secret. It gives almost any soup the right depth and kick. This dinner is simple and satisfying for any evening. Just remember to make your soup before your gin and tonic.

When you're making soup, always season whenever you're adding a new ingredient to the pot. That way, you add depth of flavor to all your ingredients.

TOMATO BASIL SOUP

Directions

In a large saucepan, heat the olive oil over medium-high heat. Add carrots, onion, salt, and pepper, and cook until they begin to soften, about 10 minutes; then add basil and cayenne, and cook until vegetables are completely soft, about 5 minutes more.

Add gin and reduce for 2 to 3 minutes.

Add tomatoes and broth and season again with salt and pepper. Bring to a boil, then reduce heat and simmer 20 to 30 minutes, or up to 45 minutes if time permits.

After allowing soup to cool somewhat, purée with an immersion blender or in a blender or food processor until smooth, doing so in batches if necessary.

If desired, stir in cream over low heat, and continue stirring until soup is just heated through. Season to taste with salt and pepper.

Servings: 6 to 8

6 tablespoons olive oil

4 large carrots, peeled and diced

1 large onion, diced

2 teaspoons salt, plus extra for seasoning

2 teaspoons black pepper, plus extra for seasoning

1 tablespoon crushed dried basil

¼ to ½ teaspoon cayenne

¼ cup gin

3 cans (28 ounces) whole peeled Roma tomatoes

1 quart chicken broth

½ cup cream or whole milk (optional)

MAKE-AHEAD MINI CROQUE MONSIEUR SANDWICHES

Servings: 24 mini sandwiches

- 1 loaf of your favorite white bread
- 4 tablespoons unsalted butter
- ¼ cup all-purpose flour
- 1 ½ cups whole milk
- Salt and black pepper, to taste
- 8 ounces tavern ham, thinly sliced (I use Boar's Head)
- 12 ounces shredded Gruyère cheese

Directions

Trim all the crust off your loaf of bread. Toast each bread slice in a toaster until pale gold.

Melt butter in a saucepan over medium-high heat. Whisk in flour. Gradually add milk, whisking constantly. Bring to a boil and whisk 30 seconds more. Remove from heat and season with salt and pepper. Set béchamel sauce aside to cool.

Spread a heaping spoonful of béchamel on 1 slice of bread to cover the surface. Top with 2 slices of ham and ¼ cup of cheese. Top with 1 slice of bread and then another spoonful of béchamel. Repeat with all the remaining toasts to make the rest of the sandwiches. When finished, top all the sandwiches with any remaining cheese and wrap individually in plastic wrap.

Refrigerate at least 1 hour. When ready to bake, preheat oven to 375°F. Unwrap sandwiches and place on cookie sheet. Bake 10 minutes. Turn oven to broil setting and broil until tops of sandwiches are light golden brown and bubbly, 1 to 2 more minutes.

Remove from oven, cut, and serve immediately.

Dropping-Off-Dinner Night
(BECAUSE YOU'RE THE BEST NEIGHBOR THEY WILL EVER HAVE)

MENU

Parmesan-Crusted Chicken Breasts with Chopped Salad

Dropping off dinner for a friend in a pinch or a neighbor in need is one of my favorite things to do. There's nothing better than discovering a hot meal on your doorstep—or being the person to deliver it to those you care about.

Here is a simple yet versatile and delicious meal that everyone in the family can enjoy. Make this ahead of time, and keep the chicken warm in the oven until you're ready to deliver the meal.

The secret to tender, moist chicken is to marinate it in buttermilk.

PARMESAN-CRUSTED CHICKEN BREASTS
WITH CHOPPED SALAD

Servings: 4 to 6

For the chicken:

4 to 6 boneless, skinless chicken breasts

2 cups buttermilk

1 cup all-purpose flour

1 teaspoon kosher salt

½ teaspoon freshly ground black pepper

2 extra-large eggs

1 ¼ cups seasoned dry bread crumbs

½ cup freshly grated Parmesan cheese, plus extra for serving

Olive oil for frying

For the dressing:

3 tablespoons red wine vinegar

2 tablespoons mayonnaise

1 ½ teaspoons Dijon mustard

3 tablespoons extra-virgin olive oil

1 ½ tablespoons grapeseed oil

1 ½ teaspoons dried oregano

Salt and black pepper, to taste

For the salad:

1 large head of romaine, chopped

1 cup halved grape tomatoes

½ small red onion, thinly sliced

¼ cup pitted and sliced kalamata olives

1 seedless cucumber, chopped

1 cup crumbled feta cheese

Directions

Pound the chicken breasts between plastic wrap until they are ¼ inch thick. Place in bowl or resealable plastic bag and add buttermilk. Marinate for at least 2 hours.

Combine the flour, salt, and pepper on a dinner plate. On a second plate, beat the eggs. On a third plate, combine the bread crumbs and ½ cup of Parmesan.

Remove the chicken from the marinade and dry with paper towels. Coat the chicken breasts on both sides with the flour mixture, then dip both sides into the egg and dredge both sides in the breadcrumb mixture, pressing lightly. (You can refrigerate the chicken at this point until you are ready to cook.)

Heat 2 tablespoons of olive oil in a large saucepan and cook 2 or 3 chicken breasts on medium-high heat for 2 to 3 minutes on each side, until cooked through. Continue the same process with the rest of the chicken breasts, adding more oil as needed. You can cover them and keep them warm in the oven at 250°F until you're ready to serve them.

To make the dressing, in a medium bowl whisk together the vinegar, mayonnaise, and mustard. Whisking constantly, slowly drizzle in the olive and grapeseed oils until smooth and well blended. Stir in the oregano, salt, and pepper.

For the salad, combine all the ingredients. Toss the salad with the dressing.

To serve, slice a chicken breast and place the slices alongside a serving of salad. If you're dropping off dinner, keep the chicken, salad, and dressing separate. Your neighbors can assemble dinner when they are ready to eat.

Crock-Pot Cooking

MENU

Italian Beef on Hoagies with Giardiniera

There is a restaurant in Chicago called Portillo's that makes the best Italian beef sandwiches. It has this amazing, specially seasoned beef, soaked in gravy and topped with giardiniera peppers, all served on a crunchy Italian hoagie bun. Here I've replicated Portillo's Italian beef in a slow cooker. Finish it off with some melted provolone if you like, and enjoy this no-brainer weeknight dinner. You can freeze the leftovers and enjoy these beef sandwiches anytime.

When it comes to liquids, less is more. Slow cookers are sealed, and liquids don't evaporate the same way they do in an oven.

Keep a lid on it. Every time you open the lid, you add 20 to 30 minutes to the cooking time.

Size it right. Your ingredients should fill the slow cooker at least halfway but not more than two-thirds full.

Browning the food before you begin slow cooking is sometimes necessary.

Prep the night before. Many recipes allow you to load the pot and store in the refrigerator overnight.

ITALIAN BEEF ON HOAGIES

WITH GIARDINIERA

Servings: 6 to 8

3 cups beef stock

1 tablespoon salt, plus extra for seasoning

1 tablespoon ground black pepper, plus extra for seasoning

2 teaspoons dried oregano

2 teaspoons dried basil

1 teaspoon onion salt

2 teaspoons garlic powder

1 bay leaf

1 package (⅔ ounce) Italian salad dressing mix

2 teaspoons crushed red pepper

4- to 5-pound round roast

1 medium onion, roughly chopped

Italian rolls

Giardiniera, mild or hot

Sliced provolone cheese

Directions

In a medium saucepan over medium-high heat, combine the beef stock, salt, black pepper, oregano, basil, onion salt, garlic powder, bay leaf, salad dressing mix, and red pepper. Stir well and bring just to a boil.

Salt and pepper roast on all sides, then place roast and chopped onion in a slow cooker and pour beef stock mixture over the roast. Cover and cook on low for 10 to 12 hours or on high for 4 to 6 hours.

Remove bay leaf and shred meat with a fork directly in the Crock-Pot so it can absorb more juices. To serve, place beef on Italian rolls and add a slice of provolone cheese. Place sandwiches in the oven at 350°F for 3 to 5 minutes or until cheese is melted. Next, add a spoonful of giardiniera to the sandwiches. Spoon juice from Crock-Pot into small bowls for dipping.

Savory Hand Pies (BECAUSE YOU'RE ALWAYS ON THE MOVE)

MENU

Chicken and Swiss Turnovers

Jamaican Beef Pies

We've all had the unavoidable, guilt-ridden moment of feeding our kids dinner in the car. I know I have, anyway. But when I served these mouthwatering, savory hand pies to my kids, they were all smiles. These pies are so versatile, and you can stuff them with almost any ingredients you like. They're comforting, easy, and fun to eat, which is why kids love them. Here are two of my favorite recipes for dinner on the go and lunch for school the next day.

When making these recipes, dice the veggies and meat uniformly, so everything cooks evenly.

These can be made ahead, stored in your freezer, and popped in the oven when you need them. To make ahead, prepare the recipes but don't bake them. Tightly wrap the pies and freeze them for up to 3 months. Let them thaw 20 minutes at room temperature before baking.

CHICKEN AND SWISS TURNOVERS

Servings: 4 to 6

- 1 ½ cups shredded rotisserie chicken
- 1 ½ cups grated Swiss cheese
- 1 cup frozen peas or vegetable of your choice
- 2 sheets (17.25-ounce package) frozen puff pastry, thawed
- 1 large egg, beaten

Directions

Preheat oven to 400°F.

In a medium bowl, combine the chicken, Swiss, and peas.

Cut the 2 sheets of puff pastry in half to form 4 rectangles, and place on a parchment-lined baking sheet. Top half of each rectangle with ¾ cup of the chicken mixture.

Fold the other half of each pastry rectangle over the chicken mixture. Press edges to seal, using a fork. Transfer pies to a baking sheet, and brush the tops with the egg. Bake until golden, 20 to 25 minutes. Let cool slightly and serve.

JAMAICAN BEEF PIES

Servings: 4 to 6

2 teaspoons vegetable oil

1 onion, finely chopped

2 teaspoons curry powder

1 pound lean ground beef or ground turkey

½ teaspoon dried thyme

¼ teaspoon ground allspice

1 teaspoon salt

½ teaspoon pepper

½ cup beef broth

½ cup bread crumbs

½ cup frozen peas

2 sheets (17.25-ounce package) frozen puff pastry, thawed

1 egg, lightly beaten

Directions

Heat oven to 400°F.

Heat oil in a large nonstick skillet over medium heat. Add onion and cook, stirring occasionally, for 5 minutes. Add curry powder; cook 1 minute. Stir in ground beef or turkey, thyme, allspice, salt, and pepper. Cook until meat is browned, about 5 minutes, breaking meat apart with a wooden spoon. Stir in broth, bread crumbs, and peas; cook 3 to 4 minutes. Remove from heat.

Cut the 2 sheets of puff pastry in half to form 4 rectangles, and place on a parchment-lined baking sheet. Place ¾ cup of filling on half of one strip. Fold dough over to enclose filling. Press edges to seal, using a fork. Transfer to a large baking sheet and brush with egg. Repeat with remaining dough strips.

Bake for 20 to 25 minutes, until golden. Cut in half to make 2 triangles and serve.

Way Better than Takeout

MENU

Sriracha Pork Fried Rice with Veggies

This is a fast, one-pot weeknight meal that everyone will love, and it's incredibly easy to prepare. You can even eliminate chopping and instead use a bag of prechopped or frozen veggies from the grocery store if you like. The marinade tenderizes the pork, and the sriracha sauce gives it a spicy kick. This recipe is way better than takeout, and it leaves plenty for leftovers.

SRIRACHA PORK FRIED RICE WITH VEGGIES

Servings: 4 to 6

1 pound pork tenderloin, sliced into bite-size pieces

¾ cup soy sauce, divided

1 tablespoon mirin

2 tablespoons sriracha sauce

1 tablespoon cornstarch

2 tablespoons sesame oil

1 yellow onion, chopped

3 carrots, peeled and diced,

1 cup frozen peas (or 1 bag frozen peas and carrots)

2 eggs

5 to 6 cups cooked rice (2 cups dry)

Directions

Place pork pieces in mixing bowl. Mix ¼ cup soy sauce, mirin, and sriracha together in a separate small bowl. Add cornstarch and mix thoroughly. Pour this mixture over pork and let marinate 10 to 15 minutes.

Preheat a large skillet or wok to high heat. Pour 1 tablespoon sesame oil in the bottom. Add half the pork and stir-fry 4 to 6 minutes or until cooked through. Remove pork from wok and set aside. Repeat process with remaining pork.

Pour 1 tablespoon of sesame oil in wok or skillet. Add onion and carrots and stir-fry 5 minutes or until tender. Add peas and cook another 2 minutes.

Crack eggs into wok and scramble, mixing throughout the vegetables.

Add rice and pork to veggie and egg mixture. Pour ½ cup soy sauce on top. Stir-fry the rice and veggie mixture until heated through and combined.

Add additional sriracha if you like more heat.

The Best Modern Casserole

MENU

Blackened Chicken with Quinoa, Feta, Artichokes, Spinach, and Mushrooms

Chefs like to call this kind of cooking method the one-pot turnaround. You make everything in one dish so you can shorten cleanup time in the kitchen.

This recipe is flavorful, healthy, filling, and can be your go-to for a one-pot weeknight dinner. If you want to make it vegetarian, lose the chicken and add the spice mix to mushrooms instead. If you want to eat leftovers for breakfast, throw a fried egg on top. Once you're done prepping, the chicken and veggies cook themselves on the stovetop in a half hour.

BLACKENED CHICKEN

WITH QUINOA, FETA, ARTICHOKES, SPINACH, AND MUSHROOMS

Servings: 4 to 6

- 3 boneless, skinless chicken breasts
- 1 tablespoon blackened seasoning
- 2 teaspoons smoked paprika
- ½ teaspoon salt, plus extra for seasoning
- ½ teaspoon ground black pepper, plus extra for seasoning
- 3 tablespoons olive oil, divided
- 1 yellow onion, diced
- 8 ounces portobello mushrooms, sliced
- 1 cup chopped artichoke hearts
- ½ cup sun-dried tomatoes in oil, chopped
- 1 cup quinoa (I use Trader Joe's tricolor quinoa.)
- 2 cups low-fat chicken broth
- 1 cup chopped spinach leaves
- ½ cup crumbled feta cheese (or more, to taste)

Directions

Place the chicken breasts in a medium bowl. In a separate bowl, mix blackened seasoning, paprika, salt, pepper, and 2 tablespoons olive oil to make a paste. Slather paste over chicken to coat. Refrigerate 15 minutes.

Heat the remaining tablespoon of olive oil in a large nonstick skillet set over medium-high heat. Add the chicken and cook for 2 minutes on each side. Transfer the chicken to a plate.

Next, add the onion and mushrooms to the skillet. Cook until the vegetables are tender, 4 to 5 minutes.

Add the artichoke hearts and sun-dried tomatoes. Stir to combine.

Stir in the quinoa and broth and bring to a boil. Nestle the chicken into the quinoa. Cover and reduce heat to medium-low. (Broth should be cooking at a high simmer.) Cook for 25 to 30 minutes or until the liquid is absorbed and the chicken is cooked through.

Transfer the chicken to a plate and slice into strips. Stir the spinach into the quinoa. Sprinkle on feta cheese. Place the chicken on top and season with salt and pepper.

Fast and Fancy

MENU

Shrimp Pasta with Roasted Red Peppers and Cream Sauce

This shrimp pasta comes together in this elegant yet quick weeknight meal. The flavors blend easily, taste delicious, and make it look as if you've been slaving over the stove for hours. Fast and fancy—check.

SHRIMP PASTA
WITH ROASTED RED PEPPERS AND CREAM SAUCE

Servings: 6 to 8

1 pound spaghetti

3 tablespoons olive oil

1 pound medium shrimp, peeled and deveined

2 cloves garlic, minced

1 teaspoon salt, plus extra for seasoning

1 teaspoon black pepper, plus extra for seasoning

1 cup chopped roasted red pepper

4 plum tomatoes, diced

2 teaspoons dried oregano

1 teaspoon dried basil

½ teaspoon crushed red pepper flakes

1 cup white wine

1 cup heavy whipping cream

¼ cup chopped parsley

½ cup grated Parmesan

Directions

Bring a large pot of salted water to a boil over high heat. Add the pasta and cook according to directions. Drain and set aside.

In a large skillet, heat the oil over medium-high heat. Add the shrimp, garlic, salt, and pepper. Cook, stirring frequently, for 3 to 5 minutes or until the shrimp turns pink and is cooked through. Remove the shrimp and set aside.

To the same pan add the roasted red pepper, tomatoes, oregano, basil, and red pepper flakes. Cook for 2 minutes, stirring constantly. Add the wine and cream. Bring the mixture to a boil. Reduce the heat to medium-low and simmer for 8 to 10 minutes or until the sauce thickens. Next, add cooked shrimp, cooked pasta, and parsley. Toss together and season with salt and pepper.

Transfer the pasta to a large serving bowl. Sprinkle with Parmesan cheese and serve immediately.

MENU

Chicken Noodle Soup

The secret to my favorite homemade chicken noodle soup is making the noodles from scratch. This may seem a little daunting at first, but trust me—it's not hard! You can mix the ingredients in a cereal bowl, then roll out your dough and cut it into strips in less than 10 minutes. The amazing difference is worth the extra effort. There's nothing better than sharing a bowl of homemade chicken noodle soup with the ones you love.

Use chicken base to boost the flavor when you don't have time to make homemade chicken stock.

CHICKEN NOODLE SOUP

Directions

In a small bowl, combine ¾ cup flour and the salt. Make a well in the center. Add water, oil, and egg. Gradually work the flour into the liquid to form dough. Add more flour as needed. On a floured surface, knead the dough 2 to 3 minutes.

Next, roll out dough as thin as possible with a rolling pin. Using a knife or pizza cutter, cut dough into ¼-inch strips. Let noodles sit while making the rest of the soup. They will be ready to go in by the time the soup is done.

Place a soup pot over medium heat and coat with the olive oil. Add the onion, garlic, carrots, celery, thyme, and bay leaf. Cook and stir for 5 to 10 minutes, until the vegetables are softened but not browned. Pour in the chicken stock, stir in the chicken base, and bring the liquid to a boil.

Add the homemade noodles and simmer for 5 minutes, until noodles are cooked. Fold in the chicken, add the peas, and continue to simmer for another 5 to 10 minutes to heat through. Remove bay leaf and thyme sprigs. Season with salt and pepper. Sprinkle with parsley before serving.

Servings: 6

For the noodles:

¾ to 1 cup all-purpose flour

¼ teaspoon salt

1 tablespoon water

1 teaspoon oil

1 egg, beaten

For the soup:

2 tablespoons extra-virgin olive oil

1 medium onion, diced

3 garlic cloves, minced

2 medium carrots, diced

2 celery ribs, diced

4 whole thyme sprigs

1 bay leaf

2 quarts chicken stock

1 tablespoon chicken base

2 cups shredded, cooked chicken (1 rotisserie chicken)

½ cup frozen peas

Kosher salt and freshly ground black pepper, to taste

2 tablespoons finely chopped, fresh flat-leaf parsley

Meatless Mondays

MENU

Chickpea Veggie Burgers with Smoked Paprika Aioli

Meatless Monday is a common term these days, encouraging people to try a vegetarian dish once a week. Veggie burgers have sparked my interest because chefs are finding new and creative ways to enhance the burgers' flavor and texture. I wanted to make an amazing veggie burger at home. With lots of seasoning and chickpeas as a base, these burgers were a hit. Definitely make the smoked paprika aioli. It's a great complement to these burgers.

Zucchini matchsticks make a great vegetarian side dish that cooks up fast. The marcona almonds give the dish a great crunch, and the lemon juice gives it a refreshing citrusy bite.

If you want more heat, add a jalapeño to the mixture.

Assemble these burgers and refrigerate them for at least 30 minutes before you cook them. Can be made a day ahead.

Get your veggie burger nicely browned on both sides to hold it together and give it some crunch.

The hardest part of the side dish is preparing the zucchini. Take care to make uniform slices so they cook evenly.

CHICKPEA VEGGIE BURGERS
WITH SMOKED PAPRIKA AIOLI

Servings: 6

For the aioli:

⅔ cup mayonnaise

2 teaspoons Spanish smoked paprika

1 tablespoon fresh lemon juice

Salt, to taste

For the burgers:

2 tablespoons olive oil, divided, plus more for frying

½ onion, diced

3 cloves garlic, minced

1 seeded and minced jalapeño (optional)

1 teaspoon ground cumin

1 teaspoon coriander

¼ teaspoon chili powder

1 teaspoon salt

½ teaspoon pepper

1 can (15 ounces) chickpeas, drained and rinsed

½ cup panko bread crumbs

1 egg, lightly beaten

2 tablespoons minced, fresh cilantro

6 hamburger buns, split and toasted

Lettuce and tomato for serving

Directions

In a small bowl, stir together the mayonnaise, paprika, and lemon juice. Season with salt and set the aioli aside.

In a skillet, heat 1 tablespoon oil over medium-high heat. Add the onion, garlic, jalapeño, cumin, coriander, chili powder, salt, and pepper, and cook until the onion and garlic begin to soften and the spices are fragrant, about 5 minutes.

In a food processor, pulse the chickpeas with 1 tablespoon of oil until you have a chunky paste. Next, add onion mixture, bread crumbs, egg, and cilantro, and pulse until mixture is well blended.

Gently form mixture into 6 patties. Refrigerate for at least 30 minutes.

Pour enough oil into a large frying pan to coat the bottom, and heat over medium-high heat. Add the patties and cook, turning once, until golden brown and heated through, about 4 to 5 minutes per side.

To serve, spread aioli on toasted buns and top burgers with lettuce and tomato.

ZUCCHINI
WITH MARCONA ALMONDS

Servings: 6

2 tablespoons olive oil

1 to 2 zucchini, peeled and cut into ⅛-inch-thick matchsticks with a knife or julienne blade on a mandoline (about 2 ½ cups)

Salt and freshly ground pepper, to taste

¼ cup marcona almonds

Juice of ½ lemon

¼ cup grated Parmigiano-Reggiano cheese

Directions

In a large skillet, heat olive oil over medium-high heat. Add zucchini. Sprinkle with a liberal amount of salt and pepper. Cook 3 to 5 minutes, until zucchini softens.

Add almonds and cook 30 seconds more. Once the moisture starts to release from the zucchini, the dish is done.

Squeeze lemon juice over zucchini, remove from pan, and place in a serving dish. Sprinkle with cheese and serve immediately.

INDEX FOR MENUS

C

D

N

O

T

ACKNOWLEDGMENTS

There are so many inspiring, creative people I want to thank. You have helped make this cookbook experience truly wonderful; I could not have done it without you.

I am so grateful to Dara Beevas, my publisher at Wise Ink and the most positive person on the planet. You kept everything moving forward and brought all this amazing talent together. Thank you for your support and enthusiasm to the very end.

To the Wise Ink staff—Patrick Maloney and Ceciley Pund, thank you so much for proofreading. Roseanne Cheng, thank you for sharing your marketing skills, introducing me to Wise Ink, and being such a great sounding board throughout this process. Thanks to Christine Zuchora-Walske, my editor, for your eye to all the details.

Another special thanks to my friends the Gustafsons, Williams, Paulsons, Vietzens, and Matysiks, who transformed a backyard into an outdoor dinner photo shoot/party before my very eyes. You got roped in "big time" and my cheeks hurt from laughing all night.

A huge thanks to Jay Monroe at James Monroe Design. You took a bunch of swirling copy and photos and turned them into a beautiful end product. Your easy-going personality and professionalism made it so fun to work with you. You have an honest approach to your craft and deserve much success.

Thanks to Tracy Severson, my dear friend and editor (behind the scenes), who knew exactly what I was trying to say, helped me get my words out, and spent many hours honing this cookbook.

To Jen Williams at Ampersand Design, my ever-patient, selfless friend and photographer: thank you for your tireless efforts and for staring at literally hundreds and hundreds of photos of me.

You are loyal to a fault! Your attention to detail and the amount of time you gave to this project will never go unnoticed. What a gift you are in my life.

Thank you to Isabel Subtil and Rachel Sherwood for our marathon two-day photo shoot. Isabel, your food photography is so creative and absolutely gorgeous—you have an amazing gift I hope to use again. Rachel, I now know the true talent of being a food stylist from watching you and that suitcase of magic. Bringing food to life is your unique talent. It was such fun working with you both.

A special thanks to Megan Tamte, CEO of Evereve. She has inspired me and many others and supported us to follow our passion. She is authentic and real and has a passion that radiates.

To my parents and friends, who supported me in my passion for this cookbook and encouraged me along the way—thank you for testing recipes, participating in focus groups, and giving me honest suggestions and opinions. I know you all had better things to do, so thank you from the bottom of my heart.

And to you, Krista, my dear friend and partner in crime, who I laughed with constantly in and out of the kitchen: I miss you and your bright light here on Earth.

Finally, to my family, Greg, Ben, and Olivia—you are my world. I have been blessed beyond belief with you three, and I love feeding you each and every day.